GOD STILL CALLS!

Vocation Stories of Real Seminarians

D1519649

Gerald J. Walsh
and seminarians of the
Diocese of Bismarck

International Standard Book Number: 1-893757-12-9

Printed and bound in the United States of America.

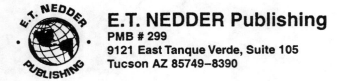

E.T. NEDDER Publishing
PMB # 299
9121 East Tanque Verde, Suite 105
Tucson AZ 85749–8390

CONTENTS

iii

FOREWORD

On December 30, 1996, I arrived at the Bismarck airport. It was the first time I had been to North Dakota. There was a certain anxiety about it all because I was chosen by Pope John Paul II to become the bishop of a diocese far away from St. Louis, which had been my home for more than 61 years. As soon as I entered the air terminal I saw the smiling face and welcoming gesture of Monsignor Gerald J. Walsh, who had been the able administrator of the diocese for eighteen months. It was only later that he explained the smile as both a sign of welcome and an expression of relief because a bishop had finally been named! I felt his support immediately and knew that I would be happy in my new home.

After the press conference the next day, I met with many of the seminarians whose stories you will read in the following pages. Monsignor was also the vocation director for the diocese and so he arranged for a gathering with these eager young men who were home for the holidays. I was delighted to be chosen as shepherd for a diocese with such promising candidates for the priesthood. In less than three years I have ordained six of these men and have seen them grow into holy and effective ministers of word and sacrament. Their straightforward stories should be a source of encouragement to anyone who is wondering whether God could be calling them to the priesthood.

Although we know that a religious vocation is a call by God and his church, we also know that the call is made known through parents, teachers, priests and other friends who touch our lives during the journey. In the 1989 statement from the National Conference of Catholic Bishops' Vocation Committee we read: "While vocation talks and literature have a moderate influence on men deciding to become priests, the two most influential factors causing seminarians to become priests are an inner calling and a priest's example." Such a priest is Gerald Walsh. You will recognize that as you read the stories of these men.

No one of us will be God's instrument in quite the same way, but it is hoped that as you read these stories you will find ways to be an encouragement to young men so that their minds and hearts might be open to a God who still calls.

+Paul A. Zipfel
Bishop of Bismarck

ACKNOWLEDGMENTS

My sincere gratitude to my present ordinary, Bishop Paul A. Zipfel, for his support and encouragement throughout the writing of this book. His comments and suggestions have been greatly appreciated and have enhanced the presentation and format of this work.

My gratitude, also, to my former ordinary, Bishop John F. Kinney, presently the Bishop of St. Cloud, Minnesota, who appointed me as diocesan director of vocations in 1991, and who has given me strong support over the years. It was his suggestion to put these stories in writing which gave me the first impetus to begin.

Of course, without the cooperation and participation of the co-authors, this book could never have been written. These young men who are now or were recently seminarians wrote their stories so honestly and completely. My respect and admiration goes out to each of them for sharing with us the personal stories of their spiritual journeys. May God's special blessing be upon them.

My special thanks to the members of the Bismarck-Mandan Serra Club, the Minot Serra Club and the State Council of the Knights of Columbus for their generous financial support. Without their assistance it would not be possible to provide every bishop and vocation director in our country with complimentary copies of this book. May God bless you for this help.

And at last, my deep gratitude to Marge Grosz, editor/director of publications for the Diocese of Bismarck. Marge, in her own generous way, gave hours of her own time to proof read, edit and prepare the material of this book for publication. Much of the easy flow of words and phrases is due to Marge's great skill and expertise. Again, may God bless you.

DEDICATION

I dedicate this book
to my beloved parents,
James and Magdalene Walsh,
the first directors of my vocation,
and to all vocation directors the world over!

With gratitude to Our Blessed Mother, Mary,
Seat of Wisdom, the Mother of all
seminarians, past, present and future.

PREFACE

During the seven years of my work as diocesan vocation director, it was our custom to have at least one or more "seminarian outings" over a summer weekend. To one of those earlier outings we had invited some young "candidates" who were thinking about the seminary but had not yet made a commitment. After our Saturday evening meal and Evening Prayer, someone suggested that the seminarians who were present share their stories of how they came to decide to enter the seminary.

The candidates, and all of us, were deeply impressed and inspired by the candor and sincerity with which the men shared their struggles and fears. The experience was such a success that it became an annual event each summer.

Finally, someone suggested that these stories should be told publicly in print. The intention was that perhaps they might help others who are presently going through similar experiences.

The following pages include some of those stories. They are told from the perspective of the vocation director, but, more importantly, also from the experience of the person himself. Please don't think that they are just pious stories of struggling souls caught in an inescapable situation. They are serious stories but also include moments of human interest and laughter. They are also stories of good times, close friendships, personal joys and group happiness.

Our seminarians, the story tellers, are not just overly disciplined robots, stereotypes of one another or of anyone for that matter. They are all unique, each with special gifts and talents, a sense of humor and very likeable traits. They are something like all seminarians, and yet we think they are special.

While these are the stories of seminarians from just one diocese, when you read them I think that you will agree that the individual backgrounds and experiences of the men vary enough to present a real cross section of seminarians throughout our country and perhaps the whole world. Each one is unique and yet there is a thread of commonality which runs through the entire group. You will see.

My present bishop, The Most Reverend Paul A. Zipfel, and my former bishop, The Most Reverend John F. Kinney, have both encouraged me in this work. It is with their blessings and support that the seminarians and I begin this "work of love."

As one of our priests* recently wrote in his column in diocesan newspaper, "This is what impresses me most about the vocation picture in our diocese. We not only have a good number of seminarians but they are really top-notch people. I've had a chance to get to know a few of them over the last couple years and have noticed some encouraging things. They are spiritually mature. They ask the right questions of life and have a deep understanding of the role their faith in Christ makes in their lives. They are disciplined yet enjoy having a good time; they have wonderful senses of humor. They are talented in a wide variety of ways: musically, intellectually, socially. They are zealous, very much "on fire" for the Lord and his church. They are normal, well-adjusted guys and seem to understand the regular struggles each human has to face in life."

Read on and enjoy their stories.

*Fr. John Guthrie, "No More, No Less," *Dakota Catholic Action*, Diocese of Bismarck, October 1998.

INTRODUCTION.

August 1, 1998 - Feast of St. Alphonsus Ligouri

In his Apostolic Exhortation, *Pastores Dabo Vobis*, "I Will Give You Shepherds", Our Holy Father, Pope John Paul II, recalls, in those words, that wonderful and encouraging promise given to us by God through the prophet Jeremiah (Jer.5:15). It is the promise of providing Shepherds for his church. Our Holy Father goes on to say in his Introduction, "In these words from the prophet Jeremiah, God promises his people that he will never leave them without shepherds to gather them together and guide them: 'I will set shepherds over them (my people) who will care for them, and they shall fear no more, nor be dismayed.'"

We hear many negative remarks these days about priestly vocations...about the shortage of priests, and the need to change the rules. Yet God's promise remains and he has always kept his promises. There are also many who maintain that there is no shortage of priestly vocations. There is only a shortage of responses. I tend to agree with them.

From my former work as diocesan vocation director for seven years and working with young people, I am convinced that there are many sincere single men out there who are called to be priests. They pray, they struggle, they have heard that the journey is not easy and they are often lead astray. One of the great challenges of our time is to invite, encourage, inspire and support those who are being called. How do we do this? Our bishops are working hard through their program, "A Future Full of Hope" and in many other ways, to address this situation.

At the recent National Symposium on Vocations held in June of 1998, both Cardinal Pio Laghi and Bishop Robert Carlson referred to "promoting a culture of vocations" whereby an environment is created "where God's people can hear, discern, understand and respond to God's call in their life." This is a realistic and noble endeavor.

The recent news that Archbishop Charles Chaput, OFM Cap. of Denver has reopened the former St. Thomas Seminary (my alma mater) under the title of St. John Vianney Seminary to accommodate the number of priestly vocations in that area, is evidence of the re-awakening of desire in the hearts of men to serve God and his people in ordained ministry. Vocation directors are laboring hard and faithfully to attract, inspire and encourage young people to listen for God's call and to respond. It is often a thankless task. They need and deserve our support. The following pages may be one small effort in the task of doing what perhaps others have often suggested.

Basically, my purpose is to inspire vocations to the priesthood. With great respect for the whole area of vocations to religious life and lay ministry, my experience has been in the arena of working with men, young and not so young, to assist them in their journeys of faith. It is from this experience that I write, and this is my area of focus in this book.

It is my hope and prayer that the following words may be instruments of grace for someone who may be honestly searching–someone whose heart is sincerely open to God's grace. I pray that the simple stories which appear in the following pages may be the source of courage and strength needed by those who read them. Courage and strength are essential. God's grace will provide the rest.

It sounds so easy and so simple. Be not deceived. Realistically, the journey is not without hardship. Long years of education and spiritual formation can be daunting to the timid soul. If we rely totally upon our own resources, it is impossible. But "with God nothing is impossible." One of our first sources of strength is the awareness and acceptance of the fact that, "Every high priest is taken from among men and made their representative before God, to offer gifts and sacrifices for sins. He is able to deal patiently with erring sinners, for he is beset by weakness and so must make a sin offering for himself as well as the people. ONE DOES NOT TAKE THIS HONOR ON HIS OWN INITIATIVE, BUT ONLY WHEN CALLED BY GOD AS AARON WAS." (Heb. 5:1-5)

In this spirit of trust, most of us who are priests have found the courage to say 'YES' each day to our priestly celibate life. And it is in this same spirit that we find the grace to surrender again and again to a loving and gracious God who generously cares for us and loves us as we are, while challenging us to be better.

It is also in this spirit that we find our joy and happiness in serving God's people and we discover over and over again what our vocation is all about. At the same time, we live constantly in the great mystery which is our life and our calling, ever grateful for the privilege of sharing so deeply in the divine life and work of the Triune God, living each day in the wonder "at the marvels God has wrought." If it works for us it will work for others who are being called. We must not lose faith in our young people. This is God's work and it is important that we believe that.

Many great and outstanding spiritual books have been written by learned scholars and wise and holy people about priestly vocations. Many works of deep inspiration and devotion are available to us these days. Do we need another one, we may ask? Perhaps not. Perhaps so. It seems that there may be a need for this work at this time in our lives. I certainly do not pretend or presume to have all of the answers to our vocation needs. Other vocation directors may have better and more effective suggestions for programs which they have tried and which work for them.

My prayer is that this book may be of assistance to some, and hopefully to many. It is dedicated to those men, young and old, who are discerning their possible call to Catholic priesthood. It may also be useful to others who work in this field. Perhaps spiritual directors, confessors, pastors and other vocation directors, who are the real unsung heroes in this labor of love, may find these pages, these stories, helpful in their ministry. I do not know. Nevertheless, that is my prayer. I do know this. It is all in the hands of God, and as before and always, Jeremiah reminds us, HE WILL GIVE US SHEPHERDS. That's his promise!

✛ ONE ✛

"Why Me, Lord?"

One of my favorite verses found in the Psalms is the line which says, "Funes caeciderent mihi in amoena, et heretitatis mea perplacet mihi." (Ps. 15:6). This verse, loosely translated, says, "The lines have fallen to me in pleasant places and my good fortune pleases me."

As I look back over 44 plus years of priestly ministry, I marvel at how God has worked in my life. As a young farm boy from North Dakota, I was a most unlikely candidate for a vocation to the holy priesthood, at least I thought so at the time. I do not mean by that statement to minimize the deep and active faith of my dear Catholic parents, but I was beset with a number of physical weaknesses and allergic difficulties almost from the first days of my life. Somehow, as often happens, the grace of God triumphed. And so, after graduating from high school and attending one year of college, I entered the seminary to begin my journey. This decision had the full support of my family and the priests and sisters of our parish.

The seminary years were long and sometimes difficult, but the grace of perseverence and many prayers from family and friends helped me complete my seminary formation and education. I was ordained a priest on May 19, 1955, and began my priestly ministry. Never in my wildest dreams did I expect my life to be filled with the variety of priestly experiences which have been my good fortune to receive. Indeed, "the lines have fallen to me in pleasant places and my good fortune pleases me" and God has been very good to me.

I do not know why I was chosen to be a priest. I only know that I live daily in the awe and wonder of it all. A wise priest once told me not to question why for there is no answer. Just be grateful every day for the gift and privilege of serving God in this special way. Some days I serve more eagerly and devoutly than others. It all depends on me...God's grace is constant...my response to it is not. With St. Paul, I am completely aware that "in weakness power reaches perfection. And so I willingly boast of my weakness instead, that the power of Christ may rest upon me." (2 Cor. 12:9-10) Again, as with Paul, God's grace is sufficient.

In March 1991, after 36 years of priesthood and the privilege of serving in almost every possible form of priestly service in the diocese, I was invited by my bishop to serve as the diocesan director of vocations. "God works in mysterious and strange ways," I thought, as I raised a number of objections and reasons why this "was not a good idea" for a 63-year-old priest to undertake.

Bishop John F. Kinney, our local Ordinary at the time, in his wisdom and, what later seemed to have been a real inspiration, simply said in reply to my objections and concerns, "I think this is of the Holy Spirit."

What can one say in reply to such a statement? "God is in his heaven and all is right with the world" as St. Teresa would say. It wasn't long before the wealth of my priestly experience of over 36 years (at that time) began to make its mark. The candidates began to come. They came slowly at first, then with a steady flow as one by one young men and some not so young, discovered a tugging at their hearts and named it "Jesus." I soon discovered that I had become a "facilitator of grace" in the awesome mystery of God's involvement in the lives of these men. I was humbled. I was inspired. And I was certainly challenged. I stood in awe and wonder of God's personal presence in our world as he individually and personally chose, called

2

and invited each man by name. Through it all I discovered that I loved being a priest more than ever.

It was not long before I realized that, as a director of vocations, I was something like a conduit or a connector, if you will, between the soul of the candidate, the one being called, and Jesus Christ, the one calling. Obviously, some relationship already existed, but I learned that once the connection is made and there is real life, i.e. grace - flowing through the "conduit," (the vocation director) he must step back and let the Lord Jesus do his work. That process, which may take months or even years, is the building up and the developing of a deep and personal relationship by Christ Jesus with the object of his choice. It is a relationship of love and finds its foundation is daily prayer, especially the celebration of the Eucharist. It has to be this way. There is no other.

This is what I call, "The Moment of Grace," and from that point on the vocation director "facilitates" the response of the one chosen. This response, on the part of the chosen, is given only by grace and through the strength and encouragement received. The vocation director must be the main source of that support. He must be careful not to "get in the way" of the love and trust developing and growing between the soul of the one chosen and the Lord Jesus who calls. The director is there, as needed, to play his small part in the great drama and mystery of "vocation," as it unfolds, the "call" and the "response." Then there comes a time, and it always happens, when his presence and usefulness is no longer needed. He must realize and accept this and not be disturbed when it happens. He has played his part. He has fulfilled his role. There are others who will be waiting for his touch. And if he is a willing instrument, Jesus Christ will use him again and again in the divine choice of his ministers.

The following pages contain accounts of the meetings, interviews, moments of discernment, journeys, struggles, joys, doubts and decisions of the men I have been privileged to work with these past years. Most of them are still on their journey toward priesthood. In some cases, however, they are also the stories of the moment of ordination and early priesthood. They are all stories of grace. They are also stories of fears, tears and surrenders. Each one is unique and yet there is that constant thread of God's involvement in each story.

They are stories of souls caught up in a love affair with a gracious and loving God–a God who chooses certain souls to serve him in priestly service. These are souls who know that they do not and cannot merit such a choice, but are generous enough to willingly offer their lives, like Mary, the Mother of Jesus, in a "fiat" of obedience. They are souls who soon learn the need for the grace and courage of daily surrender and the deep spiritual joy which comes from that embrace.

They are stories of faith. They are stories of confidence in him who calls and who sustains each of us in our vocations. They are stories of doubt and of questions--of deep prayer and desire.

They are stories of men who are weak enough to be priests because they realize that their strength is only in him. These are men who feel caught between what the world offers them, which can be very attractive, and what God is calling them to do. The competition is often staggering.

Some are the stories of generous and holy men who felt called and who responded in good faith but later discovered that their vocation was not to priesthood. They are the stories of some who tried seminary life and found their answers to be other than what they expected. Their stories are also important and we need to hear them, for not everyone who enters the seminary is ultimately ordained. That is one of the purposes of seminaries-- to assist men to find answers to their questions about their future life and God's plan for them. They, too, have our sincere respect, affection and prayerful support as they now continue their journeys toward other vocations.

I am deeply grateful to our seminarians and young priests who have given consent to collaborate in this work of love. I rejoice in the honesty with which they tell their individual stories of grace. It is our collective hope that these stories may serve to assist and inspire other men, both younger and older, who may feel the call but struggle with their response. It is our sincere prayer that these stories may be instruments of grace for others who hesitate to see God's hand in the tugging at their hearts and give then the courage to surrender as each of us has done.

I believe that it is "of the Holy Spirit." I believe that there is a new awakening in the hearts and souls of men, both the young and the older, to the voice of God. Often that voice, that call, is drowned out by the noise around us. I believe now is the time for "sharing the wealth" and reaching out to those who feel that they are all alone in their struggle to find God's place for them in this world. I believe that these stories, personal and private as they sometimes are, should be told. And may the Holy Spirit, who has been the inspiration and reason for all that has happened in my life, and in our diocesan vocation program during these past "SEVEN YEARS OF PLENTY," guide us and direct us as we begin this good work "for the greater glory of God and the salvation of souls."

⁙ TWO ⁙

The Process

"The next day John was there again with two of his disciples. As he watched Jesus walk by he said, "Look! There is the Lamb of God." The two disciples heard what he said and followed Jesus. When Jesus turned around and noticed them following him, he asked them."What are you looking for?" They said to him, "Rabbi, (which means teacher) where do you stay?" "Come and see." He answered." (John 1:35-39)

Before the individual stories of our men are read, it might be helpful to outline briefly in the next few pages how a vocation to the priesthood develops. The following steps are what I have experienced in the lives of those who are called. Although it may be true that no two experiences are exactly alike, I think that most vocation directors would agree that most young men go through something like the following.

At the outset, every man who finds himself attracted to the priesthood finds himself attracted to Jesus Christ. He discovers that he wants to know more about this man Jesus. And Jesus says to him in subtle ways, "Come and see." It is also from his own personal ideals and basic understanding of life and its purposes that this attraction arises. "What must I do to share in everlasting life?" (Lk 18:18) is a serious question in the hearts of most young people. It is especially present in the hearts and souls of one who strives to live a virtuous life and seeks holiness with daily effort. He develops a sense of his own goodness and an awareness of God's interest in him.

This labored beginning is the start of a special relationship with Christ. Deepened by daily prayer and a daily effort to avoid sin, this special friendship continues to grow and the young man learns that whatever his youthful religious education has been, he now wants more. He is hungry to know Christ. He is fascinated by things holy. He discovers his identity in the church and perhaps begins, for the first time ever, to really live a conscious spiritual life.

He may not identify it as a "spiritual life" but it is usually at this point that he needs to talk to someone and it is usually a priest. He seeks direction. He seeks virtue. He sincerely wants to be a saint, and for the first time, perhaps, he admits to himself that Christ may be calling him to service as a priest. As overwhelming as that thought can be, he looks about himself and, with the support and encouragement of a kindly priest in whom he has confided, he comes to the conclusion that, yes, he, too, could be that. The journey has begun.

It is also at this time that the candidate becomes painfully aware of his own personal sinfulness and his unworthiness in even considering such a high calling. It is extremely important that he be encouraged to continue his search and overcome his feelings of not being good enough. Sin needs to be recognized and admitted. But sin can be forgiven and overcome. Christ does not call saints, but sinners, and we all share in that state to some extent. Support, understanding and prayerful encouragement are very necessary at this time or the candidate, whom the Lord may truly be calling, will give up and the vocation is lost.

Now is the time for the candidate to seek the advice and counsel of a good spiritual director and a regular confessor. Proper spiritual direction is essential for continued spiritual growth and peace of soul.

As those first steps are taken on the journey toward priesthood and the fulfillment of the call, the candidate begins to seriously consider the virtues necessary for the life he is to live. Eventually he learns that at some future time in the course of his formation, he will be asked publicly to practice two special virtues and both demand a public response. They are obedience and chaste celibacy. He must learn to live and practice each day these virtues along with all the others.

The vocation director needs to address these virtues head on with the candidate. In some of the very early discussions, the candidate needs to know what the church expects of him. He needs to know the obligations which will be his in this area. It is not fair to "surprise" him with a later explanation of these commitments. He wants to know and has a right to know honestly and completely what the life of a priest entails. How does one live obedience and chaste celibacy all of one's life? The answer is in "learning" how. The seminary is the place to do so. Let's take a look at each of them.

The first virtue is *obedience*. At a precise moment in the rite of ordination to the diaconate and priesthood, the candidate is asked by the bishop if he promises obedience to him and to his successors. This is a most solemn moment--a public statement--calling for a completely free and sincere positive response. Moving toward this solemn moment, the beginner in the spiritual life must start to live obediently, first of all to Christ by answering the Lord's invitation, and then to the church by listening to his bishop and his vocation director as they lead and direct him day by day.

One of the candidate's first acts of obedience takes place when he shares his thoughts with another and admits that he feels called by Christ to priesthood. He may not be conscious of this as an "act" of obedience. It is, however, a response to grace which has been given freely by Christ. From then on it is a series of moments of obedience, a "configuring and conforming" of one's soul to that of Jesus Christ whose obedience to the Father led him to the cross. Obedience is not an easy virtue. Jesus says, "HE WHO WILL NOT TAKE UP HIS CROSS AND COME AFTER ME IS NOT WORTHY OF ME." (Mt 10:38)

Simply put, the practice of obedience is listening for, recognizing and responding to the impulses of grace. We may call this process "hearing the voice of Christ." This voice will come to an individual in a variety of ways and the response at times may be without effort. At other times the response is made only with pain and struggle. Jesus Christ speaks to us in many ways. It may be the voice of the bishop, the vocation director, the seminary, the church, but always it is the voice of Christ. The candidate must turn to the bishop for final proof that he is hearing the voice of Christ, for the Lord speaks most clearly through his bishops who are the successors of the Apostles.

Early on the candidate must ask himself, "If I do not listen and heed the voice of my bishop, to whom do I listen for direction?" Ultimately it is the voice of the bishop which will call the candidate to holy orders in the name of the church. At that moment his vocation becomes real.

There are those who would say that celibacy is the most difficult virtue for priests. Although it is not easy, it is my conviction that complete obedience is even harder. Those of us who have lived priesthood for decades will tell you that as difficult as celibate chastity can be, it is the virtue of obedience which is the hardest to live totally and consistently. Again, but for the grace of God, many of us would stray.

Let's talk about *chaste celibacy*. Our basic understanding of this requirement for ordination in the Latin Rite of the Roman Catholic priesthood, is that the priest may never marry. This is true. At the same time, the state of chaste celibacy means much more than that. In our world and culture where passion, drugs and sex often dictate behavior, especially of the young, it is not easy for candidates to think of a lifelong commitment to celibacy. How does one keep such a long commitment? How does one survive in our present sex-crazed world without failure?

A private and personal visit with a new candidate regarding the expectations of celibate chastity is absolutely essential for the man's

9

peace of mind. This should take place very early in the process of discerning a calling to priesthood. He will have many questions about this issue–questions which he, perhaps, will not articulate and yet they weigh on his heart. He needs to know what his responsibilities are and will be in the years ahead. The vocation director must be very sensitive regarding this subject. Understanding, compassion and encouragement are extremely necessary, but the most important attitude is one of openness and complete honesty. The entire question of life-long chastity and celibacy can be the critical point of a man's decision about whether or not he chooses to enter the seminary, or whether the vocation director thinks he should.

This can be especially challenging if there has been a past history. It is important for candidates to know that past sexual activity does not necessarily exclude them from a priestly vocation. It is important for them to know that chaste celibacy is not impossible, and that they, too, can learn to live this virtue successfully. This, however, can only be accomplished with the grace of God. They must come to respect this state as a gift and a charism. They need to be trained and formed in this virtue day by day in order to live out their sexuality in a mature and positive, celibate way.

Our seminaries are doing an admirable job in teaching the total picture about chaste celibacy and also challenging the candidates to such a life. They are teaching our men how to live this gift as mature adult males and how it pertains to the total mystery of priestly vocation. Recently, The St. Paul Seminary in St. Paul, Minnesota, published an excellent book on this subject entitled, *Formation for Priestly Celibacy, A Resource Book.*

Not long ago, one of our transitional deacons, who was ordained a priest in 1999, wrote the following words in a letter to me. "The big event this week was a sexuality workshop from the folks at St. Luke's. We talked about lots of things, from pretty-simple to pedophilia. What I appreciated most was the treatment of sexuality as an expression of God's desire that we act relationally, as the

Trinity does--Father, Son and the Holy Spirit. Sexuality, as it was used this weekend, means 'the entirety of your energy for being with others.' That includes a lot of stuff, huh? Sexuality gives, and takes, a lot of our energy. I once heard someone say 'that's why sexual drives are so powerful...they are what draw us out of ourselves into relationships.'"

In his exhortation, *Pastores Dabo Vobis*, Our Holy Father says, "Since the charism of celibacy, even when it is genuine and has proved itself, leaves man's affections and his instinctive impulses intact, candidates to the priesthood need an affective maturity which is prudent, able to renounce anything that is a threat to it, vigilant over both body and spirit, and capable of esteem and respect in interpersonal relationships between men and women." Chap. V #44.

The commitment to a life of chaste celibacy should never be considered simply a negative way of life. A healthy attitude is that it should be a positive, joyful, living out of one's sexuality. In fact, a vocation to priestly service includes the need for passion. This may sound like a contradiction when speaking of celibate chastity, but in the best sense of the word, seminarians and priests must be passionate people–passionate for Christ and his church. Chaste celibacy must be "life-giving."

If seminarians will discover a real value in this gift and plunge into the mystery of how it is all a part of God's plan for their lives as priests and for the life of the church, they will seek it with all their heart. Then it will become a tremendously important part of their daily life and ministry. Then it will not be a negative thing....a "lifeless" way of life. It will be--it must be-- a positive, active, incarnational way of life. Otherwise it will be simply a lifelong burden and an impossible cross.

Archbishop Harry Flynn of the Archdiocese of St. Paul-Minneapolis, recently wrote in his weekly column (*The Catholic Spirit*, Oct. 22, 1998), "We often see celibacy in the solely negative terms of self-denial, whereas St Paul saw it as a virtue in which the unmarried person 'can devote himself to the Lord's affairs' (1 Cor. 7:32). ...If celibacy is a way of devoting oneself 'to the affairs of the Lord,' then it must be a way of loving. Indeed, celibacy is a love 'which knows no rivals and a joyous disposition of heart for pastoral service.' (*Instrumentum Laboris*, 35)."

Candidates need to know that they will have help. They need to be told that it is possible. They want to know that they can do it and that we trust them to be able to live chaste celibacy for the rest of their lives. They want our prayers and our support. They want validation of their own prayer life and their devotion to Our Blessed Mother. We need to tell them that without a strong daily prayer life rooted in the Eucharist and a deep personal relationship with Jesus Christ, it can't be done. In him is our strength and they soon discover that as well. The joy of knowing that they can do it, with his help, makes all the difference in their response. Now they are ready to enter the seminary and begin the journey.

And now we are ready to hear their stories, first in my words and then in their own.

THREE

Father Austin Vetter and Father Patrick Schumacher As I Recall Them

At the time of my appointment as vocation director for the diocese, there were seven young men studying for the priesthood for our diocese. Among them were Austin Vetter and Patrick Schumacher. Both of these young men were students in second theology at the North American College in Rome at the time and I had never met them. I had heard their names mentioned and heard about them as seminarians but they were strangers to me.

Patrick and Austin had graduated from their local high schools and then journeyed to Fargo to North Dakota State University for their college work. Their stories will tell you about those early years in college. I only know that soon after beginning their college studies they were touched by God and felt called to be priests. Moving slowly through the usual struggle of doubt and wonder, and encouraged by the right people at that time in their lives, they both entered Cardinal Muench Seminary in Fargo to begin their seminary formation.

They did not know each other when they entered the seminary, but as they continued their seminary course in Fargo and prepared for theology, they became close friends. As they completed their college work, the question of an appropriate theologate for them arose. The bishop suggested the North American College in Rome and they both agreed. So in the fall of 1989 Austin and Patrick made their way to Rome to prepare for the holy priesthood.

It was a day in mid June of 1991 that I had my first meeting with Austin and Patrick. Although I would not officially become the diocesan vocation director until July 1 of that year, I had been invited to a luncheon at the bishop's house for Austin and Patrick. They had just returned from Rome for the summer following their second year of theology.

I remember being at the bishop's residence a bit early that day. It was customary at that time for visitors to enter the residence by way of the Chancery entrance on the lower level. We staff members all knew that. Others did not. Austin and Patrick came to the front entrance and rang the bell. As I was coming up the stairs to the upper level where the dining room was located, I noticed them at the door. I went to the door to welcome them and they, realizing their error, were already making their way to the rear of the building. I called them back and welcomed them at the front door. I remember it well because my first impression was so favorable.

Austin and Patrick were suitably dressed in suits and ties and looked very much the part of the formal seminarian coming to the bishop's table. Austin had a big smile on his face. Patrick was more reserved and serious. They are both still that way. Like most of us priests, even close friends, they are quite different in personality but so similar in gift and dedication.

That summer I came to know and appreciate each of them. Both were and are very bright young men, each with special gifts and singular talents, similar and yet different. Both are deeply religious and devout young men in love with the church and in love with the priesthood. They are good friends and both possess outstanding leadership ability. Austin talks more. Patrick, as mentioned before, usually is more quiet and reserved.

14

Austin is the youngest of 12 children in a deeply Catholic family with traditional values. He was raised on a farm near Linton, North Dakota. He is a priest now and is honored and cherished by everyone in his family. He lives his faith each day in open and obvious ways. He has served as a teacher of religion for the senior class in one of our Catholic high schools, where he was both a challenge and a challenger to each student in his classes. He is also a good pastor in the best sense of the term. He is generous and loving and is highly regarded by his people. He is sensitive to their needs and serves them with great care.

Patrick is also a priest now. They were ordained together on the Feast of Sts. Peter and Paul on June 30, 1993. In his own special way he also lives his faith firmly with no apologies. He is also a teacher of high school religion in a Catholic high school and pastor of a challenging parish. In both areas he excels and is loved and respected by both his students and his parish members.

Patrick has had to face and address some very difficult parochial issues in his young years of priesthood and pastoral ministry and has done so wisely and appropriately. He has discovered that real leadership and wise counseling are some of his special gifts and he uses them well. He, too, comes from a deeply Catholic family and is served well by the faith of his loving parents and siblings.

Having walked with these two young men, now priests, through the last years of their theology classes and spiritual formation, I have come to know and respect them deeply. Present for their ordinations to diaconate and priesthood, I found it to be an honor and a privilege to present them to the Ordinary as candidates for holy orders. It was also my singular privilege as administrator of the diocese in 1996 to give them their first pastoral appointments. They have not disappointed me or the church. My confidence in them and their future is secure and full of hope. The church in the Diocese of Bismarck has been, and will continue to be, well served and blessed in their ministry.

Father Austin's Story...In His Own Words....

It has now been six years since I was ordained a priest and recalling my vocation story has proved to be quite fruitful. As I look back over my life, it seems so obvious to me that God was calling me to be a priest and yet as I was going through those years it was anything but obvious.

My family was a great seed bed in which my vocation flourished. I always knew that to be a priest or a religious would be a great thing as far as my family was concerned. I grew up in a wonderful family. Being the youngest of 12 children had it advantages and its disadvantages. A great advantage for me was that since there were enough of the others to do the work each day, I was able to go to daily Mass with my grandfather and spend time after Mass visiting my aunts and uncles. I loved to go to church with my grandpa. Many days the only people at Mass were my grandpa and me, and the priest. Those are still some of my fondest childhood memories.

Another important part of my childhood journey to God was the fact that when I played Mass at home, my mother was a great supporter. Even though we always had to share everything from food to clothing and, of course, the bed, Mom always bought me oyster crackers and grape juice so that I could have "Mass." No one else was allowed to eat them and it was one of the ways my parents showed me that they would love it if I was called to be a priest.

My name, Austin, came from Fr. Austin Herrmann, the priest who baptized me. The fact that he was also named after a priest always struck me that maybe this is how God works. As a small child, this seemed to me like a pretty good way to make priests, just name them after the priest and that was that!

As we were growing up, we always went to Mass and CCD classes. I can never remember any of us children complaining that we had to go to church. It was as basic to our family life as chores and eating meals together. I used to think that all families did these things and I was quite shocked in college to find out that this was not the case. It was also at the university that it dawned on me that not everyone my age was thinking about the priesthood.

The fact that I was thinking about the priesthood while so few others my age would even go to church was seen by me as a huge sign from God that this may be my vocation. I recall praying each night before going to bed while I was in college, "God if you want me to be a priest, just show me." My first year at college was going quite well. I was dating regularly and my classes were going well. I recall one night in April of 1986 studying for a test in computer science. I was wondering if I wanted to do this kind of work for the rest of my life. My major was mathematics but I just couldn't see myself as being all that happy doing that. I remember praying that night in a more fervent manner than I had for some time. I told God that this was it. If I did well on this computer science test, I was not going to look back. I was going to put this priesthood stuff out of my mind for good. I slept well that night and awoke for the test. That test score was the worst I had received in my life. Now I can see that I really didn't want to do well on the test. In any event, I called the seminary the next day and asked Father Gross, the rector, if I could go to school there and become a priest. I had no idea how long it took or anything. I thought that I would possibly be a priest in a matter of months.

My main purpose for going to the seminary was to be told that I was not supposed to be a priest. I wanted that nagging in my heart to stop and I thought that going to the seminary would rid me of the thought of the priesthood. I wanted to be married some day and I wanted children, so I knew that I had to deal with the priesthood sooner rather than later. I couldn't imagine getting married with the issue unresolved. I gave the seminary one year to settle the issue for me.

Well, the seminary settled it. My time in the seminary are treasured days. I learned much about myself and the church which I loved so dearly. Once I got to the seminary I gave myself totally to the formation program, trusting that God would work through the priests

17

on the staff. At the end of the first year, I asked Father Gross if I could return for another year. Of course, he said, "yes."

I was the happiest I had ever been and the sense of peace from doing God's will was a constant presence, even during the difficult times in the seminary. I am so grateful to my family and to Almighty God for allowing me to share in the gift of priesthood. What a wonderful, beautiful and humbling way of life God has chosen for me!

Father Patrick's Story...In His Own Words....

I still cannot believe, after six years to the day of my ordination, that I am a Roman Catholic priest. My name is Father Patrick Adam Schumacher and I am a priest for the Diocese of Bismarck. I am honored to write this reflection on the story of my vocation to the priesthood for the Reverend Monsignor Walsh. As my vocation director and diocesan administrator who assigned me to my first parish as pastor, never forgetting his generous assistance during my first challenging year as pastor, the monsignor (whom I call "IL MONSIGNORE!!" with unfettered respect) has been one of the many "keys" (to use a pastoral emphasis) in my life. So let me begin as I began.

I still cannot believe, after six years to the day of my ordination, that I am a Roman Catholic priest. During my years of high school in Williston, North Dakota, and during my first year at North Dakota State University in Fargo, I can say without hesitation that any thought of being a priest was very remote (actually close to nonexistent; there was not *ANY* thought) in my mind. I wanted to be an auto mechanic. Then I wanted to be a locomotive engineer. Then I wanted to be a lawyer. Then, while taking the required philosophy courses for my political science degree and going to Mass regularly at the Newman Center on the NDSU campus, I thought about being a priest - for the second time.

18

The first time was when I was eight years old in the third grade when I began my career as an altar boy at Mass. The thought was familiar to me, thanks to my mother and father who faithfully raised me in the Catholic faith. Then, as I entered junior and senior high, the aspiration left me. Then, when I met a couple of other "key" (there's that word again) priests, the whole idea began to haunt me.

A call to be a priest, I have discovered is something you can never lose; although it may be possible to "duck" it for an entire life-span. I know men who have "ducked" it.

Other "keys" are Father Phil Ackerman and Father Dale Kinzler, priests for the Diocese of Fargo. In Fargo at NDSU, I met them and considered being a priest for the Diocese of Fargo. I also met Bishop James Sullivan, the Bishop of Fargo. As I struggled and prayed and "discerned" and, quite simply, just wanted this whole feeling to go away, this bishop and his priests were very important in directing the entire course of my life, back in 1986. Father Ackerman finally said, "Patrick, if you don't go to the Diocese of Bismarck as a priest, who will?"

Directing me back "home," I then met the late Father Michael Mullner. Father Michael was a fantastic priest who loved the church and every day of life. Father Mullner drove to my hometown of Williston (with his Russian Wolfhound "Sebaca" in the backseat) to take me to lunch and talk about the priesthood. I will remember that meal in the Plainsman Hotel forever. I signed up to enter Cardinal Muench Seminary for one year for the very simple reason that I could not go through life wondering what God would have done with me if I would have given him an opportunity. I sincerely felt a desire to "clear up this whole thing" and move on in life. And move on I did, but not according to my plans.

After completing my BA degree after three years at Cardinal Muench Seminary, Bishop John F. Kinney sent me to the Pontifical North American College for theological studies. After four years, I was ordained in 1993 under the imposition of hands and through the words of Bishop Kinney, another "key" in my journey.

After a fifth and final year in Rome to complete my S.T.L. degree in moral theology, my journey in the pastoral life of the priesthood began.

I will end as I began. I still cannot believe, after six years to the day of my ordination, that I am a Roman Catholic priest. Now I will add, I have never regretted making that decision, or I should say that I have never regretted giving our Lord the opportunity to work in my life!

There are many vocation stories in this book and I have heard, quite literally, hundreds during my eight years of seminary life. Vocation stories are all so different, but they are all the same: "Key" priests and bishops, a struggle, a surrender, then the challenge of being a "doer" of God's Word. The United State Bishops, in their document, *The Challenge of Peace,* collectively write:

> "To be a Christian....is not simply to believe with one's mind
> - but also to become
> a doer of the Word....even if that leads to the path of persecution
> and the possibility
> of martyrdom."

I would add.."...even if that leads to the priesthood...!"

You do not need to really know anything more about me. I am just like you. My summer jobs at Pizza Hut, refinishing wood gym floors, painting concrete floors, etc. are not important. I even joined the Navy and I was Lt. (junior grade) for a short time of active duty. I have had girlfriends and one girlfriend in particular, who had to hear this story as well. My family, my history, my work, my relationships, my different details - tell the same story. This, however, is important. I am just like you.

If you have even a remote thought about being a priest, can you go through life wondering? Can you not give Our Blessed Lord a chance, even if it be remote, to work through you, the seminary staff, and our ultimate goal of God's people? Give Our Lord a chance! Lend him, if not your entire life in the beginning, at least a finger for him to grasp!

I once asked Father Robert Laliberte, in 1987, if he thought God was calling me to be a priest. He answered, "I don't really know. But if you *are* called to be a priest, you will first begin to think about it!" Father Laliberte, there is another "key."

I believe that all Catholic men should go to the seminary. Not all would become priests but all would undoubtedly undergo a transformation of life in the Catholic faith. We need good priests and we need good laymen. In the seminary, you cannot lose anything in life. The seminary produces both.

I would like to leave you with a quote from Pope John Paul II. This quote, ironically, is from 1987 and I used this quote on my holy card upon ordination. I thank you, I bless your decision, and I leave you with these words:

> *I am deeply grateful to God for my vocation to the priesthood.*
> *Nothing is more important to me*
> *or gives me a greater joy than*
> *to celebrate the Mass each day and to serve the people of God*
> *in the Church. This has been truly so since the day of*
> *my ordination to the priesthood.*
> *Nothing has ever changed this , not even the*
> *event of being elected Pope."*

John Paul II, September 15, 1987

FOUR

Father Leonard Savelkoul As I Recall Him

The revival of the Order of the Permanent Diaconate in our Catholic Church has given many men, especially married men, a whole new understanding of and opportunity for sacred ministry. In most dioceses it has become a tremendous source of ordained ministry in Catholic parishes and institutions, and a great form of support and assistance to priests and pastors.

When the approved Rite of Permanent Diaconate was first made available, a number of older single men became interested. Some of them were men who, at one time, had considered a vocation to the priesthood but now thought that they were too old to pursue that goal. They opted, instead, for the Permanent Diaconate. Some of them were actually ordained as permanent deacons and then reconsidered and discovered that the Lord was now calling them to priesthood. This became more and more common as older men were being accepted by bishops as candidates for the priesthood.

Leonard Savelkoul was one of those men. He had grown up on a farm at Lansford, North Dakota, and, like so many of our candidates, had attended and graduated from the high school in a small rural community. He was not familiar with a great deal of travel and had spent his growing up years at home with his family. It was during those years, attending Sunday Mass with his devout Catholic parents and his brothers and sisters, as well as his experience with family prayer and devotions in the home, that Leonard often thought of a possible vocation to the priesthood.

He did not know many priests but his deep Catholic faith told him that this was how vocations began: a tug at the heart; an attraction to priestly life and ministry; a desire to know, love and serve God in special ways; a genuine care for the needs, especially the spiritual needs, of others. All of this was part of Leonard's experience.

After graduation Leonard enrolled in the nearby State College and after four years, he graduated with a degree in education. This would be a way to serve others. He would become a teacher. He was not interested in teaching in large schools. His small town background kept him very comfortable in small town schools. Leonard taught high school classes in several small town schools for 28 years. He was appreciated and greatly respected. He seemed to have found his niche.

In spite of his contentment with his life and the work he was doing, from time to time that old "tug at the heart" would return. Leonard would dismiss it with the thought that he was getting too old to begin over again. He was not "eligible" anymore because of his age. The years rolled by and then, all of a sudden, he learned about the revival of the Permanent Diaconate and the possibility which it offered to older men, married or single.

This seemed to be just what God wanted him to do. He could continue with his teaching career and also serve the church as a deacon in his local parish. Leonard enrolled in the diaconate program and went through the three year program of formation. He loved the program and made new friends among the other deacon candidates. Although he was the only single candidate, he was well received and felt at home with the others.

Leonard seemed to have found his vocation. His great sense of humor, his deep faith and natural preaching abilities, his dedication to service and his genuine goodness made him a prime candidate for ministry. He was ordained a permanent deacon along with his classmates and was very happy in that life.

Throughout his diaconal formation, it became more and more obvious to his director and to the bishop, that perhaps Leonard's vocation was not only to the diaconate but also to priesthood. Older men were now entering seminaries all over the country and there were now special seminaries where older man could go for their spiritual and academic formation.

It was in June of 1991, at the ordination ceremony of another permanent deacon, that Bishop Kinney took Deacon Leonard aside, along with the vocation director, and said, "I want you in the seminary this fall." I happened to be the new vocation director present so Leonard and I began to visit about his future. The more we visited, the more we both agreed that this seemed to be God's will. Leonard was happy as a deacon but priesthood seemed even better.

We began the paperwork. The journey to priesthood had begun. We had only a few months to complete the registration. At times we wondered if this was supposed to be. As is often the case, roadblocks kept popping up. Delays in obtaining records, misplacing of important papers on the part of the seminary staff; obtaining copies and re-submitting documents all took time. The deadline was approaching. Finally, a couple of frantic phone calls assured us that Leonard was, indeed, registered and was expected for the fall program.

It was not easy for Leonard to give up his teaching job. It was difficult to know that there would be no monthly pay check coming in for the next four years. It took great faith for him to let go of his career, his many friends back home, and start all over again at age 54. Returning to the classroom as a student instead of a teacher was very hard. And yet, he did it all and did it very well.

The four years went by very quickly and Leonard was a very good student. He made new friends in the seminary and discovered the joy of a deep spiritual life. At last he had truly found his real vocation and many years since he first felt that tug at his heart, he knew that this is what Christ wanted him to do.

Father Leonard was ordained a priest on May 23, 1995. He is now a good pastor of a small parish with two missions. He does not mind being known as a "belated vocation".....he loves his priesthood. The journey was long and "different" but he is now "home" and he knows, at last, that this is where he belongs.

Father Leonard's Story...In His Own Words....

At age 62, many of the priests my age are counting the years until retirement and making plans as to where they will live out their "golden years." I, on the other hand, am still one of the "new kids on the block" having been a priest for only four years. You might ask, "How did this come about?"

As I look back on my life, I realize I have always had a deep love for the church and the idea of priesthood was always somewhere in my mind. I remember as a child playing Mass in the barn on our farm at Lansford. I was always the priest and my three brothers and two sisters (one my twin) were the congregation. Crackers were our Communion bread.

Even though I attended public school for both elementary and high school, I received two weeks of religious education each summer taught by the Benedictine sisters. After high school graduation, I started college at Minot State University, but left after two years. I then worked as a truck driver, a farmer and an oil field worker. After three years of this, I decided it was more important to complete my education, so I returned to college to finish work on my degree in history and industrial arts.

I then realized that what I really wanted to do was teach high school kids. I made the right decision because I remained in education for 29 years. And I loved every minute of it! I taught one year at Hazelton, six years at Balta, and twenty-two years at Burke Central High School in Lignite. I still keep in touch with many of my former students. In fact, 34 of them attended my ordination. What an affirmation for me!

To me, teaching was not just a job, but a way of life. It was my vocation. These students were "my kids." I not only took pride in their academic accomplishments, but also great interest in their extra curricular activities. I urged them to play better on the football field or the volleyball court. I helped them sort out their plans for the future. I also tried very hard to instill moral values in them, telling them to avoid drugs and premarital sex. I counseled many of them and provided an adult role model for those who had no other role model in their life.

Although my students filled the greater part of my life, I was also involved in many community activities and organizations. Another interest that I enjoy is photography. This has been a hobby since high school and continues to this day. Many times I provided the photos for graduating classes in high school and continued this during my years in the seminary.

My Catholic faith has always been very important to me. Over the years I served my parish as a lector, lay minister and a trustee.

In the mid 1980s, I heard about the revival of the permanent deacon program in the Catholic Church. Here was an opportunity for me to serve as an ordained minister. I completed the three years of deacon formation and was ordained in May 1988. As a permanent deacon I officiated at a number of baptisms and weddings of family members and former students. But the tug at the heart to be a priest was still there, and it surfaced from time to time. Now, however, it seemed to be stronger than ever.

Over the years many people questioned me about a possible vocation to the priesthood. Parishioners at Bowbells often asked, "Why don't you become a priest?" This was in the 1960s and at that time there seemed to be a surplus, so again the idea took a back seat.

In 1987, Fr. Blaine Cook spoke at Mass in Lignite, a liturgy I was deaconing. His homily focused on "second career vocations." Fr.

John Pfeifer turned to me and said, "Now is your chance. Take advantage of it or forget about it." I heeded his words and took advantage of it.

I remember in 1988 asking a student, Shannon O'Connor, "Can you see me as a priest?" He said, "Yes." I couldn't believe it! He was at my ordination and First Mass.

There were others who also thought I belonged in the seminary. At the permanent deacon ordination in 1991, Bishop John Kinney and Msgr. Walsh came up to me and maneuvered me away from everyone else. They both said they wanted me to enter the seminary. I had one year left to teacher retirement. I promised the juniors I would not retire until the next year when they graduated. I kept that promise and spoke at their graduation.

That summer found me pulling up stakes in Lignite, leaving family and friends and heading off to Sacred Heart School of Theology in Hales Corners, Wisconsin, that fall. I was used to the single life and living alone. Now I was living in a dorm with a hundred other people!

Sitting on the other side of the desk was also quite a change for me. Term papers, drop tests and taking notes weren't new to me. I was used to laying these on my students. Now I was the recipient. I also experienced the anxiety of getting grades from my professors. What a change!

All in all, I truly enjoyed my seminary days in Milwaukee. Sacred Heart is a seminary for delayed vocations, so I was with many men in my age bracket. I was ordained a priest on May 23, 1995, at the Cathedral of the Holy Spirit in Bismarck. At the time I was the oldest permanent deacon and oldest person to take advantage of a second career vocation. Bill Cosgrove now holds that distinction. I was the last priest ordained by Bishop Kinney before his move to the St. Cloud Diocese.

The four years since my ordination have gone fast. I am now the pastor at the Church of St. Bridget in Parshall and the missions at Makoti and Plaza. I love being a priest and a pastor. I enjoy officiating at baptisms and weddings, and especially at the sacrament of reconciliation. To be a good pastor, one must like people and that comes naturally for me. I truly enjoy people and especially working with the youth.

I look back on my life and realize that God moves in mysterious ways. That tug of the heart was always there. We often think, dreams can't come true. I'm living proof that they can if you really want them to. I've found that being a teacher and being a priest work well together. I'm still a teacher, but in a new way.

So, if you feel that tug of the heart, remember, it's never too late.

FIVE

Father Thomas Richter
As I Recall Him

There is a book somewhere entitled, *The Family That Overtook Christ*. I do not remember the author but that title might be applied to the family of Victor and Mary Richter and their 14 children. As I begin this story of a bright, athletic devout young man, I want to say that the Richter family has been an inspiration to countless folks who know and love them.

My story begins long before Thomas James was born on October 26, 1967. I knew Tom already in 1947 because I knew his father, Victor Richter at that time. Victor was in the seminary with me for at least three years, both in what we called in those days, minor and major seminary. Victor was from a very staunch German Catholic rural family and had a number of brother and sisters. Children were valued in those days and the bigger the family the greater the wealth. The John Richter family was rich indeed–rich in faith and family values which Victor learned and practiced very well.

At any rate, Victor discovered that his vocation was not to priesthood but to marriage. He left the seminary and found a wonderful Catholic girl to marry. Her name is Mary. Mary was also from a large Catholic family. She had three uncles and three aunts who were Benedictines. Now you know why Victor and Mary were a perfect match. They practiced their Catholic faith with great respect and devotion, and their home was a perfect seed bed for vocations. Therefore, no one was surprised when young Tom decided to enter the seminary. Later his brother, David, would follow him. His story will also be found later in these pages.

Tom was a "middle child" in the family of 10 boys and 4 girls. With all of those brothers, some might think that Tom's motivation for entering the seminary was just to get away from his brothers. That could be understandable. They were devout, prayerful people, and, yet, they were also typical boys. They worked hard on their dad's farm but they also had great fun.

Like most brothers, they were into great competition.....always trying to outdo one another. In school they were good students but their love was athletics, especially wrestling. Strong, muscular farm boys are no match for "town kids." Several of the Richter boys, including Tom and David, won state championships on the wrestling team of the Catholic high school where they studied.

The brothers were also something of a "party people" and loved their beer and an occasional cigar. Dating was common and they were popular, handsome young men. All of this was part of Tom's life as a teenager but he will tell you in his story how God began to tug at his heart. He "wrestled" with the thought of a vocation for some time and finally, after earning a degree in electrical engineering at the university, he felt compelled to give the seminary a try.

It was there that I first met Tom Richter. As I assumed the office of vocation director in the spring of 1991, I decided that one of the first things I must do was to become acquainted with our seven men in the seminary. I made a trip to Fargo to visit the college men at the seminary there. It was an afternoon in April when I arrived and Tom Richter was walking down the main corridor of the seminary when I arrived. I still remember vividly his pleasant welcome and the nice visit we had.

On that occasion we had opportunity to get to know each other and I was very impressed by Tom's sincere and humble approach to his vocation. He still was not convinced that God was calling him but he was giving it everything he had, as was his way of doing everything. Tom had hair then. Now that he is a priest for two years, that has pretty much disappeared. Tom had some rough spots in his character to smooth over in those days. Now he has acquired social graces and attitudes which suit him and serve him well in his pastoral ministry.

At the same time, Fr. Tom still enjoys a good time. He is sought out by his peers and has many loyal friends. He is still a tease at times and still competes but mainly with himself. He is now the pastor of a small parish with one mission and doing excellent work for the Lord. He recently took on the duties of parish administrator of a neighboring parish and its mission. His people love him and he serves them with devotion and sensitivity. He also teaches at one of our local Catholic high schools and is admired and deeply respected by the students he teaches. He has had a very promising and successful three years of priesthood so far and is sought after by many groups and organizations for public speaking engagements and spiritual direction.

As vocation director I enjoyed working with Tom throughout his years in the seminary, first at Cardinal Muench Seminary in Fargo and then four years at the North American College in Rome.

Tom was always open to my suggestions and direction. He was always eager to comply with what was expected of him as a seminarian and young priest. Sincere in his care and concern for others and generous to a fault, he is an outstanding young priest and my affection for him is deep and genuine. Fr. Tom Richter has a promising future ahead of him. His devotion to Our Blessed Mother and our Lord in the Blessed Sacrament is fervent and sincere. He lives his faith and his convictions openly and without pretense. He is a positive example of goodness in our world of sham and phony negativity. One of his co-teachers has put it well..."Father Tom is so real!" That pretty much says it all! Read on and see if you don't agree!

Father Tom's Story...In His Own Words....

Sharing the story of my road to the priesthood always causes me a little anxiety. I am not sure about the reason for that. I have shared it dozens and dozens of times. Each time seems to be different than the one before. I want to be precise, exact and clear, but it usually does not turn out that way. This much is clear: it was not my idea. I did not want to be a priest. It was not something I thought of or desired. It was God's idea and his desire...and God gets what he wants.

FAMILY:

I must begin with my family. They had a big part in nurturing me in the life of faith. Mom is a true servant of God and of her family. She is the anchor and provides the stability for our family. I cannot begin to illustrate all that Mom has done. But I will try. She is the mother of fourteen children, and, besides doing the million and one things a mother of so many children must do, up until the birth of the eleventh child, she milked sixty cows practically every morning of her life. Now that I am older, I can see that being alone in the barn during that time was her refuge. She used cloth diapers for all fourteen children. She used a wringer washing machine through the birth of her last child. She cooked and served more food than most small cafes. In the midst of all this, she never complained and even considered herself blessed. She was, and still is to me, a sign of great strength and a living example of a true servant of the Lord.

Mom has a gentleness that every mother dreams of. As a small boy I was often sick with ear infections. In the middle of the night I would awaken Mom, crying and telling her how bad I felt. Even though she would lose valuable sleep, she never showed me anything less than deep compassion. She would get up and doctor me until I was once again sleeping soundly. Looking back, it is amazing how much I believed in my mother. Her presence alone brought me security and peace. I will always be grateful to God for her.

Perhaps the best way to describe Dad would be to say that he is a "character." It is impossible to have a dull moment when Dad is around. He is full of life. He does everything full speed; he says what he thinks; he is 100% German. He is less openly affectionate than Mom, typical of the German male. It was rare for Dad to give us warm compliments or affectionate praises, but at every social event he bragged to everyone else about how great his children were. Although it was difficult for him to express it, Dad has always had a soft heart for things that really matter. It was not rare to see Dad shed tears while listening to tragedies on the nightly news.

Dad is a devoted man. He has always been deeply devoted to the Catholic faith, his wife, his family, his farm and his friends. In fact, he has childhood friends from the years he spent in the high school seminary with whom he still gets together with several times a year. Mom and Dad compliment each other very well. They always held up high standards when it came to practicing our Catholic faith. Sunday Mass and the sacrament of reconciliation were simply a way of life for our family. Not once in all the years when we were children at home do I ever recall any one of us every saying anything like, "Dad, I don't think I am going to Mass this Sunday." This was not even an imagined possibility. The sacraments were like oxygen to our family...without them one cannot live.

Our family was very involved in our small parish of a hundred families. It was not uncommon on any given Sunday for the Richter family to be well represented in the liturgy: Dad would read, Mom would play the organ, two of us boys would be servers, and two more Richter boys would be ushers. I used to joke with Dad that it bothered him that the priest was not a Richter. So I became one!!

The family rosary was another common spiritual exercise in our family. Mom would light a candle for the rosary. We all faced the crucifix in the front of the room. Dad sat in the very back of the room, behind everyone, in his recliner, while making the rest of us kneel. We would try to find a pillow or cushion to put under our soft knees. Dad would say, "It doesn't hurt that much. You don't need cushions." Of course, he said this with his feet up on the recliner. Mom would kneel with us in silent revolt against Dad. Then we would begin. We mentioned things we wished to pray for and then Dad led all the way through the first mystery. After that it was open game. The tension mounted. Anyone six years old or older was a candidate to lead the next mysteries. It was scary for a seven year old to try to lead the rosary in front of four older brothers who are waiting for you to make a mistake so that they can chuckle at you. Usually somewhere between the Our Father and the ten Hail Marys one of us would accidentally begin with the second part of the Hail Mary or lose our breath in the middle and make a strange noise. That was all it took for the rest to start giggling and laughing. If this was not enough to cause tears, the ending usually did. After we finally finished with the rosary, the Memorare and the Sign of the Cross, all of the little kids would make a dash to be the first to blow out the candle. As expected, one would beat the others, blow out the candle, and thus make all the others cry, so Mom would stand there and light the candle over and over again allowing each child to blow it out. She was so patient.

The amazing thing about all this is that we still laugh about it and we still pray the rosary. The rosary proved to be an effective reminder to me as a child to be a person of prayer, and that prayer is something that we do inside and outside of church.

My vocation to be a priest seems to have had deep roots. Three brothers and three sisters of my maternal grandfather became Benedictine priests and sisters. So, having three great uncles as priests and three great aunts as sisters, gave me much exposure to the priesthood and religious life. In addition to this, my father also spent seven years in the seminary: four years of high school and three years of college. I still joke with him that he was in the seminary longer than I was. Discerning that his vocation to was to married state, he never lost his affection for the seminary and his friends there.

Every other year, Crosier Seminary, where Dad had studied, sponsored an alumni gathering. We would load up our station wagon with kids--I'm not sure how many there were at the time but the car was full--plus suitcases, and head to Onamia, Minnesota, for several fun-filled days. We kids looked forward to this more than anything else each time we went. We all have great memories for those trips were positive experiences--and they all happened at a seminary.

We lived in the country and attended the local rural public grade school, so we went to CCD until high school. I fought with Mom and Dad like every other kid about going to CCD, but I must say that I enjoyed the challenge of being able to know my prayers and all the answers to questions the teacher asked. For some reason it was important that I knew my religious beliefs and was able to defend them. Even as a kid I liked talking about religion and morality.

There were a few people outside of my family whom God put into my life at crucial times and who had a great impact on my future decisions. The first person is my brother-in-law, Leland Vetter. I was in the seventh grade when my older sister, Mary Ann, married Leland. It was an important time in my life as I was beginning my teenage years. I always felt a special bond with Leland. Looking back, I think it had to do with faith. I found Leland to be a persuasive and inspirational man. He is convicted, has an uncommon common sense, is happy and funny. He has high ideals, and at the same time he understands weakness and how insane kids can be. I do not think I have ever had a conversation with Leland that somehow did not eventually involve God, the church, morals, heaven or the real questions of life. Whenever Leland came to our house, within minutes he would have the whole family laughing and shouting at the top of our lungs about some topic. (In our family, we do not listen to the one who speaks first but the one who speaks loudest!) It was great! Leland and I were able to talk about things in a way that my older brothers and I were not able to do. I think God used Leland to make me think about important things at a time of my life when it was easy to get focused on unimportant things.

The other person was Father John Kuhn. He was sent by God to our parish precisely at the time when I began to think about the seminary. It was not rare for Father Kuhn to give a similar homily more than once. One would not consider him to be a nuanced man. He often covered the same points week after week. But he was a man of deep passion and conviction. He was 100% a priest from the "old school." He was nearly seventy years old when he came to us and yet he had a kind of "fire in the belly" that you would expect only in a young priest. He was a devout man of prayer. His style and identity are exactly what I needed to be inspired at that point in my life. Many Sundays I would leave Mass longing to have what Father Kuhn had-- his single hearted commitment to Jesus.

INTERIOR MOVEMENT OF GRACE: CHILDHOOD

To follow God, there must there be outside influences, but most importantly, there must be interior movements, the stirring of the heart, the touch of God. God speaks to us in the silence of our hearts. Unfortunately, it is sometimes difficult to hear the silence....but it speaks loudly.

The first sign of God's desires at work in me that I can recall was before I started school. It was something simple but I think it was real. It was my job to take out the garbage each morning after my brothers and sisters went to school. We had two garbage barrels on the farm, one for things to be burned and the other for cans, glass jars, etc. One day when I had separated the garbage into the two groups, I found a missalette among the items to be burned. My father was a lector at Mass and so he often brought a missalette home to practice the readings, and then threw them away when they were expired. I saved the missalette and told Mom that we should not burn it in the garbage because it was something we used at Mass in church. It did not seem right to me. Mom said that it was okay to burn it but she didn't convince me.

Now I burn missalettes all the time. Although this innocent respect for missalettes may seem trivial and even scrupulous, I have come to see that as an example of God, giving me a sense of the sacred in my youth. I was given an awareness that there was a realm, or a reality, that was beyond earthly things and so there was need for respect to be shown. I could not explain it, and most would say it was one of those common, cute, innocent things kids do. But I think a dash of grace was involved. The fact that it left a deep enough impression on me that I would still remember it twenty-five years later seems to support my belief.

The next moment of experienced grace that I recall was when I was in the early years of school. It happened on only a couple of occasions. It was in the fall; the air was fresh and I was playing outside in the trees and the fallen leaves carrying my football when I would experience a deep peace. It lasted for only a moment but it has left an impression in my memory. It was an experience of harmony between me and God's creation. I felt overjoyed to be alive and experienced an incredible feeling of security, like the feeling of being hugged by someone. This same thing happened one day when I was sitting at my desk thinking about the very event mentioned above.

Once again, I think that these were more than just a young boy's excitement to be outside playing, It seemed to be from something or someone beyond ordinary experiences.

My First Communion was a special day for me. My family really made me feel like the luckiest, most blessed kid in the whole world. I recall that my brother, Marlyn, called me "The First Communicant" for the whole day. I am not sure how he meant it, but I took it as an honorary title. I still remember rehearsing for my First Communion like it was yesterday. The dear sister who taught us CCD--and I am ashamed that I cannot remember her name--walked us through the ceremony the Sunday before the big day. At one point she gave each of us an unconsecrated host to hold and look at. I was ecstatic. For years I had wanted to be able to touch and receive the host. One of the reasons I remember it so well is because I could not resist the temptation and I soon ate the host. Shortly after eating it, sister asked us to give them back so that we could practice going through the Communion line and receiving. I was embarrassed to have to tell her that I ate it, especially when I discovered that I was the only one.

Probably the most remarkable thing surrounding my First Communion is this story. The Andy and Marge Schweitzer family have been friends of our family from the very beginning. They have ten children and we have fourteen, so there was always a Richter and a Schweitzer together. Toby Schweitzer was the finest friend any young boy could want. He was mine and we still stay in touch today, although never enough. In normal circumstances we were willing to almost lie, cheat, steal, and pillage in order to stay overnight at one another's houses. Even milking cows was enjoyable when Toby was helping me.

The weekend after my First Communion, Toby asked me to stay overnight at his house in town and then his mom would drive me home to our farm on Sunday afternoon. Not having a big world view as an eight year old, I did not realize that more than St. Hildegard's of Menoken had the Eucharist. I thought that if I stayed at Toby's I would not be able to receive Holy Communion that Sunday, so I did the unthinkable....I told Toby that I could not stay at his house because I wanted to receive the Eucharist. He spent the next few minutes trying to convince me that I could receive Jesus at his church too. Finally, he was successful.

These are nice memories. This was the work of God in my little soul. I am convinced that this awesome excitement for the Eucharist which was in my heart as a little boy was one of God's precious gifts given to prepare me for the priesthood.

TEENAGE YEARS:

Unfortunately, I was a pretty normal kid, so when I contracted the disease called "the teenage years" I had pretty much all of the symptoms that most teenagers have. My interests were sports in junior high and more sports and dating during my high school years. However, I do think that there was something a little different about me than was true of most of my male classmates. I desired to know my religious beliefs better than my peers. When a religious question came up my peers would turn to Tom. I served Mass until I was about fifteen years old. Throughout my whole life I have never gone through a phase in which I skipped Sunday Mass or did not regularly practice the sacrament of reconciliation.

Lastly, I have always had a profound affection for the Catholic Church. I would like to think that I now have a reverent, healthy love for the church, but in the past I think I may have had a dash--a big dash--of self-righteousness or elitist sentiment in this regard. Nevertheless, I have had this passionate defense for the church since I was a boy. It is kind of like the difference between a boy's willingness to fight for his girlfriend or the neighbor girl down the street. The passion for the former is much greater than the latter. Giving me this passion and affection for the Catholic Church, I believe, is another way in which God prepared and formed me for the priesthood.

As I have said, I have nine brothers, four of whom are older than I am. I think it is natural to want to be like one's older brothers, at least that was my case. This was especially true with regard to my brother, John, who was next oldest to me in age. John is a good man. He has a heart of gold. It would be difficult to find a man who would say anything negative about John. He was a close brother to me in my teenage years. John was also the finest, most humble wrestler that our high school has ever seen. He was a North Dakota state champion, which was the beginning of a long line of Richter brother wrestlers. My brothers, Dave, Jerry and I also became state wrestling champions. My brother, Patrick, whose qualifications to be a state champion were much greater than mine ever were, contracted mononucleosis just days before the regional tournament of his senior year and was not able to participate. He would have been a great champion.

Throughout high school, my one goal was to follow in John's footsteps and become a state champion. In fact, each morning of my senior year, as I drove the 22 miles from our farm to school, I would pray the rosary for the intention of becoming a state champion. I smile in embarrassment over my intense self-concern and vanity as I think about it now. With millions of people starving, being murdered, being abused, not receiving an education, not knowing Jesus Christ, living in poverty, and on and on, I simply prayed for my own self-glorification morning after morning. Nevertheless, I did become a state champion. I reached my dream. But a couple of weeks after the tournament, after reaching all of my goals, after attaining the apparent object of my happiness, not much was different. I had the thought, "This is it? This is all? There must be more." Through this experience I became aware that there must be more to life than what I was seeking. I felt unfulfilled.

COLLEGE YEARS:

Toward the end of my senior year, "The Call" began. Every morning I would wake up and think about the seminary and the priesthood. I did not want to be a priest, but it was there each morning for my four college years. I did not know what to think. I was not sure if God was inviting me and calling me to be a priest and I was resisting, or if some altruistic desire in me was urging me to be a priest and God was resisting. It was a confusing time, especially with all of the distractions and temptations that college life offers.

Throughout those four years of college, God was active in many ways, but his major work was to hound me. He never let up. He was the "Hound of Heaven" and he was perfectly comfortable with letting me be unsatisfied and disappointed when I got what I thought would make me happy. He was trying to nurture in me a desire for more--for things that do not pass away--and to lessen my appetites for the gifts of this world

I attended Bismarck State College for two years and then North Dakota State University in Fargo for two years. I studied electrical engineering and received my bachelor's degree from NDSU. It just so happens that Cardinal Muench Seminary is also in Fargo. Austin Vetter, the baby brother of Leland, my brother-in-law, was already in the seminary. Austin and I were altar boys at the wedding of my sister, Mary Ann, and his brother, Leland. Throughout the years we had become good friends and remain so to this day. Because of our friendship, I often visited Austin at Cardinal Muench Seminary and even spent a weekend there. It was a blessing to have a friend there with whom I could identify. One of my greatest obstacles to overcome was the thought that I was "too normal to be a priest." Knowing that Austin and I were a lot alike and that he was happy in the seminary was helpful in my discernment. Austin's choice to enter the seminary was an inspiration to me and gave me the courage to follow.

This very morning I celebrated Mass with a deacon. The deacon was David Richter, my younger brother who will be a priest in one more year. You will find his story in another chapter of this book. But I must relate this story: One year when I came home from college for a school holiday, I wanted to spend the evening with David and my buddies. None of us were in the seminary at the time. However, my buddies wanted to go to the bar and Dave was only nineteen years old. Being prudent, Dave thought it would not be a good idea for him to go but I talked him into using my old driver's license, which he finally agreed to do. It just so happened that an employee knew that Dave was underage and turned him in to the manager. The police came and Dave was handcuffed and taken off to jail. We easily got him out and there were no serious consequences. However, since it would probably be published in the local newspaper, I decided that we needed to explain things to Dad before I left for college again.

He was on the tractor, feeding cattle. I went and rode with him as he worked. This was not something that I normally did so he knew that something was up. He finally asked, "Now what?" I proceeded to tell him the whole story. He maintained his composure for a few moments but then let me know what he thought. After several minutes of parental admonishments he ended with a prophetic command, "You damn idiots have no business in a bar. You should be in the seminary where you belong!" Shortly thereafter I joined.

SEMINARY YEARS:

The work God performed in the seminary was to reveal to me my gifts. It is amazing to me how many years can go by without knowing oneself or one's gifts. Before entering the seminary, I did not realize many of the gifts with which God had blessed me. The seminary years were a time for me to discover many of them. It was a time of great growth, self-discovery, self-acceptance, and affirmation. It was also a time to develop a prayer life and a close relationship with our dear God.

Bishop Fulton J. Sheen was popular among some of my friends in the minor seminary and so I began listening to him. He had an impact on me, especially his unconditional commitment to the daily Holy Hour in Jesus' presence in the Blessed Sacrament.

Perhaps the greatest grace God gave me in the seminary was the men with which he surrounded me. Shortly after I entered the seminary, our bishop appointed Msgr. Gerald Walsh as our vocation director. He was a gift from God. He was in his sixties but could water ski better than any of us seminarians. He was young at heart with a passion for life. Most importantly, he was a happy and holy priest who was deeply in love with Jesus, the Virgin Mary, and the church. He loved being a priest and he made it attractive to his seminarians.

Both seminaries I attended--Cardinal Muench in Fargo and the North American College in Rome--were blessed with impressive priests and seminarians. It was truly a grace to witness the faith, commitment and intelligence of these men. They all had one desire: to be true to Jesus Christ and his church. It was a deep blessing to live with these men. Surrounded by these men one could not help but want to serve God and neighbor.

Last but not least, I must mention one of my professors who had a profound impact on me. Father Paul Murray, O.P., was my spiritual theology teacher. Father Murray is a charismatic man. Fr. Paul was always surrounded by students hoping to get a few minutes to speak to him. He was a personal friend, retreat master and spiritual director for Mother Teresa of Calcutta.

His classes were more like retreats than lectures or lessons. Day after day he would have the entire room of students eating out of the palm of his hand, hanging on practically every word. Listening to him made all that I knew "in my head" become real in my heart. It was rare for me not to leave his classroom without my heart experiencing some sort of compunction. Besides theology, Father Murray taught me a valuable lesson. He never forced anything. He had this ability to offer teachings in such a way that one wanted to follow them. In short, it was obvious by his life that he had something precious and he made me want to have it also. He had something that I wanted. This, I believe, it what it means to preach the Good News.

SHEER GRACE:

The singular most lasting reason why I am a priest happened to me in a convent in the mountains of Italy outside of Rome. It was late September of 1992. It was the fall retreat–a seven-day silent retreat-- before my first year of theology in Rome. My spiritual director for the retreat was Fr. Hank Bertels, S.J. Up to this point my desire not be a priest was stronger than the desire to be one.

On the second day of the retreat I decided to fast. All meals were in common so all present knew if someone was fasting. Perhaps, it was a vain desire that pushed me to fast. Whatever the case, that afternoon when I met with Fr. Bertels, he asked me why I was fasting. I responded with some sort of pelagian reasoning like I wanted to get more disciplined etc.

He then asked me a direct question, "Tom, can you make God love you more or make him love you less?" I thought I knew the right answer to that question, but I kind of mumbled an unconvincing response. So Father Bertels responded with something like, "You know you can't make him love you. But you also know that he already does. So, the reason you are fasting is not to make him love you, but as a token of gratitude for the love he already has for you. Right?"

When he said those words, something happened. A person, a presence, entered me, transformed me, stole me, laid a claim on me. Physically, it felt like someone pouring warm water under my skin. Emotionally, I felt like I did when that special girl called. Psychologically, it was like being freed from an addiction; chains were broken. Wholly, humanly, it felt like I was recreated. I was a new creation. My entire view of reality changed in moments because I was confronted with the utter unmerited, undeserved, uncaused, unearned love of God. I no longer saw God as the rewarder or punisher but the God of utter mercy and goodness.

This experience is still with me, like it happened yesterday. I am a new creation. This encounter with the Spirit of God transformed me. The major changes to come from this were: My emphasis in seeking God is no longer to avoid the fires of hell, but once one tastes and sees the goodness of God, one is given the realization that he would be an absolute fool not to seek him and him alone. The other major change was that from that moment on I have been overjoyed to think that God would choose me to be his priest. He chose me. He chose me. It is sheer grace!

FROM HERE:

A vocation story never ends. In fact, ordination is only the beginning. The journey continues, but throughout the journey the terrain changes. I have always had this devotion and reverence for doctrine. I have always had the sense of duty to God in himself. Most of my journey in the past has been focused on that. Now my journey is more focused on learning to be a loving caring servant for his people. My sense of duty to God remains, but now I am acquiring a stronger sense of duty to God by serving his people.

I am also very aware that living the Catholic life is about a new life, the new life of Jesus Christ. So, the life I live and the work I do is about the life and work of Jesus Christ in me and through me. It is his life and his work. It is himself. He is my life. He is my love. He is my all. I am only an instrument. This is easy to say, but difficult to live. This is the work of God and I thank him for that. May he bring to fulfillment the great work that he has begun in me and in all those he has chosen to be his priests.

✧ SIX ✧

Father John Mathai
As I Recall Him

Some of the strongest words of Jesus appear in Luke's Gospel, Chapter 14:25-26, "On one occasion when a great crowd was with him, he turned to them and said, "If anyone comes to me without turning his back on his father and mother, his wife and his children, his brothers and sisters, indeed his very self, he cannot be my follower."

John Mathai was a happy boy in the city of Alleppy, Kerala, South India. The son of deeply religious parents, with two devout sisters and brothers, John was one of the middle children in the family. As a young boy he prayed fervently for God's will and as he grew up he became more and more convinced that God wanted him to be a priest.

John was a bright and intelligent young man. Therefore, he was sent to St. Pius Seminary in Bombay for his philosophy studies. Only the best and brightest students studied there. After finishing his philosophy courses, he began to wonder about his calling. One of his sisters was planning to be married and, in India, the parents of brides bear the heavy burden of wedding and dowery expense while the groom's parents pay very little. Since John was not sure of his future vocation, he decided to take some time from his seminary studies to work and earn some money to help his parents.

Bombay is a big city and John soon found work among the poor and oppressed. He began to take classes in sociology and earned a master's degree in social services at the same time. His work with the poor put him in contact with a priest from Kerala by the name of Father Peter Kunnalakat. They worked together for a few years and then John again felt the tug of Jesus at his heart. Through prayer and spiritual direction John came to the conclusion that God wanted him back in the seminary. His vocation, after all, was to be a priest and serve God's poor in that way.

"Turning his back once more on his father and mother, ...sisters and brothers," as Jesus requests in Luke's Gospel, John applied once again for acceptance at the seminary. He found, however, that his local bishop was no longer interested in having him as one of his seminarians and would not sponsor him for his theology courses. This news came as a deep disappointment to this young man, but made him all the more determined to seek God's will and continue on.

The next verse in Luke's 14th Chapter speaks of the importance of "taking up one's cross" in order to be a follower of Jesus. In another place Jesus says that this must be done "daily." John was not unfamiliar with crosses. This one, too, he would shoulder and move ahead, following Jesus wherever he would lead him.

The Lay Missionaries of Our Lady is a community of devout people who offer their lives in the service of the church in missionary lands. John learned that this group would accept him for one year and sponsor him in the seminary for that time, until he could find a bishop and a diocese to accept him. The Lord continued to lead and so John entered St. Pius Seminary for theology classes but lived in the slums of Bombay with three of his classmates for one year. This was an experience of poverty and suffering which would always serve to remind John of the blessings which those days provided as he identified with God's poor in their own sad condition.

In the meantime, John's friend, Father Peter, had been sent by his archbishop to work in the Diocese of Bismarck for a period of three years. Was the Diocese of Bismarck a "missionary diocese?" Did it qualify as such for John's purposes as a member of the Missionaries of Our Lady so that he might apply for acceptance there? To the people in Kerala, India, where vocations abound, Bismarck was, indeed, a "missionary diocese." Father Peter began to set things in motion for his friend back in Bombay.

It was in early spring 1994, that Father Peter approached me about "a seminarian in India" who was "looking for a diocese." This seminarian, according to Father Peter, was completing his first year of theology and would be ready for ordination in just three more years. After an interesting discussion with me, I promised Father Peter to do my best for his friend. After approaching Bishop Kinney and receiving his approval, I wrote to John Mathai in Bombay and asked for basic information; i.e. family background, religious and education background, work experience, personal history, etc. I also inquired about the strength of his vocation and his interest in coming to the United States to serve here as a priest.

John responded promptly and efficiently. I was greatly impressed. The more I corresponded with John and requested forms to be completed, applications to be filled out, and documents to be sent to me, the more impressed I became.

Finally, I had to hear his voice. It is not easy to make phone calls to India, especially when seminarians there do not have private phones and are often moving from class to class to lunchroom, etc. throughout the day. The time difference is another big factor and cause for concern. Father Peter was most helpful in suggesting that I make the phone call late at night which would be morning in Bombay and thus would be easier to contact John. After three attempts to reach him, I finally make contact and heard the voice of this young man who had become very special to me through correspondence. We had a brief conversation, mostly about his plans to come to this country in May. It was great to speak with him and to hear his command of the English language and note the sincerity in his voice.

Our correspondence continued, and with the approval of Bishop Kinney, I made arrangements for John to come to our diocese and to spend the summer in Bismarck. This would help him become acquainted with us, see our local area, and get to know our priests and seminarians. April 30th was to be the day of his arrival.

Father Peter came to Bismarck from his parish to be present for John's arrival. He and I went to the airport on time and the plane landed. We watched with anticipation as each person disembarked. At last the plane was empty and there was no John. Fearing that he was lost in the Twin Cities, I frantically made phone calls to the Northwest Airline Customer Service in St. Paul. They did not have him on their list of passengers for that particular flight and did not know of anyone by the name of John Mathai who might be flying to Bismarck that day. Fr. Peter and I finally went home dejected and wondering where John might be. It is a long way from Bombay to Bismarck. Where could his plans have gone astray?

After a fitful night, I was at my desk the next morning at 9:00 a.m. when my secretary said that a phone call had come in from John Mathai and that he was at the airport in Bismarck. I drove to the airport in haste and found this young man from India waiting in the terminal. I saw him from a distance as I entered and walked toward him and as soon as I said, "John?" he came running and flew into my arms in an embrace as though we had known each other for years. This was the beginning of our friendship and John's journey to priesthood as a seminary student for the Diocese of Bismarck.

After a summer in Bismarck living at the Cathedral of the Holy Spirit, John entered the Pontifical College Josephinum in Columbus, Ohio, as a student in second theology. After three years at that seminary, John was ordained a priest for the Diocese of Bismarck on June 19, 1997. His love of God and his church and his zeal in wanting to serve God's people has brought him to this "missionary diocese."

Here he will offer his priestly ministry with the same deep love and affection which has sustained him through the many crosses he has had to carry in following Christ.

Father John has not "turned his back on his father and mother, sisters and brothers" to forget them or to shun them. He, however, has "left all things to follow Christ"...and while his family remains in India, he will always be part of them and they are a big part of his ministry. Their deep faith and abiding love have formed an attitude and a disposition in their son, Fr. John, which makes him the loving and gentle pastor which he has become. Even at a great distance, they are very much a part of who Father John Mathai is. May they be blessed forever for the gift of their son to us.

Father John's Story...In His Own Words....

From India With a Smile...

"We are instruments of God's mercy, love and peace," is what comes to my mind as I reflect on my vocation to the priesthood and priestly life. No matter where and who we are, God effectively uses us, to reach out to people. All that is needed is our complete trust and surrender to his plans. I guess that summarizes my life.

I am currently the pastor of Holy Trinity Catholic Church in Hettinger and its two missions, Sacred Heart, Scranton, and Sacred Heart, Reeder. I am originally from India. In fact, I am the only priest from India (at least for the time being) who is incardinated into the Diocese of Bismarck. In other words, my commitment to the Diocese of Bismarck is permanent.

I come from a normal, middle class family in India. I was born on May 22, 1966. Both of my parents are still living. I also have two brothers and two sisters, along with three nephews and four nieces, and another one on the way. All of my siblings are married and settled in India. So that leaves me as the only one from my family here in the

50

United States. As things are going now, I will soon call North Dakota my home.

The first seed of my vocation was planted by my parents. Their simple faith and trust in God was an inspiration to serve God as an altar boy and a lector before joining the seminary. I always found them beginning their day with a prayer before the picture of the Sacred Heart and our Blessed Mother.

The manner in which priests are able to reach out to people was the encouragement for me to pursue my vocation to the priesthood. After receiving a bachelor's degree in psychology, I went on to study philosophy. During that time, my family was going through a crisis, so I thought it was my obligation to help them. Therefore, I took a break from my seminary studies.

Having received a master's degree in sociology, I worked two jobs as a guest lecturer in one of the colleges and as a program coordinator for social work activities in the college of social work in Bombay. While on this job I was actively involved with the rehabilitation and relief of the victims of the communal riot in Bombay. This instilled in me a deep desire to serve the people who are suffering and reach out to them. I was convinced that in the moment when people are really in despair and hopeless, God reaches out to them. He uses you and me to reach out to them.

That conviction prompted me to rejoin the seminary. With some difficulties, I was back to St. Pius Seminary in Bombay and continued with theology studies. During the first year of theology, I lived with fellow seminarians in a slum in Bombay. This was part of a program introduced at the seminary during that time. Sharing one room with three and living with the bare essentials was very hard in the beginning. But it taught me to be content with what we have. More than that, it taught me to share what I have with others.

I wanted to serve the Lord where priests were needed most and I was looking for a bishop to accept me. Fr. Peter Kunnalakat, who served the Diocese of Bismarck in Kenmare for three years, got me in touch with Msgr. Walsh, vocation director for the Diocese of Bismarck.

I clearly remember the day Msgr. Walsh phoned me in Bombay. I was very scared and did not know what to say. His natural affection and love, however, reached out to me miles and miles away. That enabled me to say "yes" to coming to Bismarck without much difficulty.

I will never forget the moment he received me at the Bismarck airport. The affectionate hug made me feel that we had known each other forever. I don't know whether I was Irish in my last life, because ever since he has supported and encouraged me like a father.

Having arrived in the United States on June 2, 1994, I visited with Bishop John F. Kinney, and he accepted me into the Diocese of Bismarck. I spent a couple of months at Cathedral Parish and in the fall entered the seminary.

Continuing my studies at the Pontifical College Josephinum, Columbus, Ohio, helped to prepare me for my priestly ministry in the United States. Having earned a master's degree in divinity, I was set to enter the field of ministry. During the summer I was back in the diocese spending time doing Clinical Pastoral Education (CPE) in Minot and served at Our Lady of Grace Church as a deacon. These experiences helped to familiarize me with the diocese, the priests and the people.

My day of ordination and First Mass in the diocese, and the Mass of Thanksgiving in India were very special moments of grace and fulfillment in my life. Though I have only been ordained a priest for two years, the number of people I have touched in my ministry makes me feel that I have been a priest for a long time. God uses you and me, if we are willing to let him.

People often ask me if I miss my family. SURE I DO! I keep in touch with them over the phone. I have met many people here who reach out to me as members of my family and I am glad to be a part of several families in the diocese. As I express my gratitude to them,

I thank God for taking good care of me. The bishop and priests of the diocese are very encouraging and I am privileged to be part of the presbyterate of the Diocese of Bismarck. People accept me for what and who I am and so I give my best to the people of God.

No matter where on earth you are and who you are, God has a plan for you and me and he is very good at executing the plans. It is good to be a priest. I am very happy as a priest and want to continue to live and die as a priest.

Keep smiling..Jesus loves you!

SEVEN

Father Wayne Sattler
As I Recall Him

When Jesus said to his disciples, "Come follow me and I will make you fishers of men," (Mk 1-17), we read further in the next verse that "they immediately abandoned their nets and became his followers." (Mk: 1-18).

It sounds so simple and so easy when we read those words today. We wonder, though, if it was that clear and uncomplicated. Didn't they have families to whom they would have to explain their absence? Didn't they have other obligations and commitments to which they had to attend before "leaving all and becoming his followers?"

What about that miraculous catch of fish in Chapter Five of St. Luke's Gospel? Two boats filled with fish so that "they nearly sank." (Lk 5-7). Then after Peter's little discourse with Jesus, "they brought their boats to land, left everything, and became his followers." (Lk 5-11). As practical as we like to think ourselves to be, we wonder what happened to all of those fish. Was it all so simple to follow Jesus' invitation in those days?

Not so today. So many attractions beckon our young people. Father Wayne Sattler was a young boy in the sixth grade in our parish school of St. Patrick in Dickinson when I first became acquainted with him. I was the pastor and would spend time in the school as duties would allow. Young Wayne was a quiet, bright little boy, but otherwise seemed quite a lot like all the others. As I recall, he caused no trouble in school and was a good student.

After moving from grade school to high school, and graduating from Trinity High School, Wayne attended college at the University of North Dakota in Grand Forks for one year. In high school he had been active in sports, particularly in wrestling, and had made a name for himself. He graduated as an honor student in his class and did well in college.

During those years of adolescence I was not aware of the interior struggle taking place in Wayne's heart and soul, his attraction to the spiritual life and his agonizing struggles to find his place in God's plan. Wayne became a very sensitive young man, possibly because of the suffering and pain of witnessing the separation and ultimate divorce of his parents. Being the youngest of four children, Wayne felt the pain more deeply than the others and turned to prayer at an early age for comfort. It was this very pain which perhaps was the reason that Wayne's heart was open to God's call.

After one year of college he entered St. John Vianney Seminary in St. Paul as a seminarian. As devout and dedicated as Wayne was that year, he was not certain of God's plan. After beginning his second year at the college seminary, he decided to leave the seminary until his life's direction would be more clear. His leadership qualities had been recognized by his peers at St. John Vianney and he had been elected student president of the seminary. It was not an easy decision for him to leave but it seemed the right thing to do at the time.

Wayne continued his study of philosophy at the University of St. Thomas and graduated with a major in that field. After working for a year, falling in love and becoming engaged, and having this experience of the real world, Wayne was torn between marriage and religious life. Again, the struggle and pain, until finally he decided that marriage was not for him. After breaking his engagement, he called the vocation office in Bismarck for an appointment.

It was in October of 1992 that Wayne made a special trip from St. Paul, Minnesota, to Bismarck to visit me. Although I had not seen Wayne for at least ten years, I recognized him immediately and we visited about many things. His question about his future was paramount and I encouraged him to let God have his way, whatever that might be.

The next few months were filled with prayer and discernment and in May of 1993, Wayne came to Bismarck to spend the summer working in a parish. This decision helped him reconnect with our diocese after being away so long and it also gave him a sense of rootedness which he very much needed. The final decision was made in June and Wayne requested a return to the seminary. He asked to be sent to the Pontifical North American College in Rome for his theology. Bishop Kinney complied and I agreed with this request. Wayne studied diligently for four years in Rome and was ordained a priest on June 19, 1997.

"Come follow me" is not an easy invitation to answer. It is only with God's grace and much personal and family prayer that the correct response can be given. Then it must be given over and over again so that each day of seminary life and each day of priesthood may begin with a "freshened YES" to what God has planned. Only then can a vocation to the holy priesthood be truly fulfilled with joy and peace. Only then can the People of God be truly served and God's glory and reign be established in our hungry world.

Fr. Wayne Sattler is presently in his second year as a parochial vicar, currently serving at the Cathedral of the Holy Spirit in Bismarck. (His first year after ordination was spent at Our Lady of Grace Parish, Minot). He is also in his second year of teaching religion classes to the seniors–this year at St. Mary's Central High School, Bismarck, and last year at Bishop Ryan High School in Minot.

His own personal story has become a rich resource which enables him to relate extremely well to the young people with whom he comes in contact. He understands their personal temptations and struggles, their doubts and fears, and is sensitive to their sincere search for God's will in their lives. His priesthood has not come to him easily and perhaps that is why he is so effective in his priestly ministry today. His total and unconditional response to the Lord's invitation to leave all and follow him continues to be his source of grace and strength.

Father Wayne's Story...In His Own Words....

"When did you decide to become a priest?" "What inspired you to make that decision?"

For all the times I have been asked these questions you would think that I might have a pat answer ready to methodically rifle back. But as quaint as these questions might sound, they are not as easy to answer you might imagine. Most people imagine that priests are priests because God gave them no other choice or desire; that somehow when we came out of the womb we are ready-made for celibacy and already had a hankering to dress in black. I wish it were all that easy, but it isn't, at least it wasn't for me.

There was no one decisive point in my life when I *"decided to become a priest."* There were no visions, no voices, just a gradual realization that my true fulfillment in life was only going to come by first denying myself, picking up my cross and following after the only person who could ever hope to satisfy the longing of my heart. Satisfying the longing of my heart, now this was the endeavor that eventually led me to discover my vocation to the priesthood. To help unravel what I mean by this, it would perhaps be beneficial to provide a little personal history.

When I was in the third grade I received the shattering news of my parents' impending divorce. For those who have been through this experience, no explanation is necessary. For those who have not, no explanation is really possible. The pain of a fragmented house left me with a heart eager to be affirmed. My parents and siblings did what they could to help this youngest child with a difficult transition, but looking back it is evident that we were all struggling in our own ways to fill the void left by this break in the family bond. Success became an obvious pacifier as was the exclusive attention of the "significant others" I eventually dated. Fortune seemingly smiled upon me. Throughout high school I had my share of honors and accolades in sports, speech, drama and leadership activities. And the girls with whom I was able to spend extended time alone helped to remedy my craving for individual attention.

Despite being motivated by the normal influences of adolescence, success, peer approval and the attention of pretty girls, a deep moral awareness was already being engraved in the recesses of my mind. At the same time I would have to admit that there certainly were times when I did my best to keep this awareness right there in the recesses.

Throughout some difficult years, my mother was constant in her efforts to raise her children with an awareness of our need for God. We never missed church on Sunday and great pains were taken to ensure a Catholic education. Mom's faith always helped me to see God's hand in the most trying situations. Between her and my middle brother, Tracy, I was always encouraged to seek refuge in God. Looking back, it was indeed his embrace that consoled me through the nights and valleys of a rather insecure adolescence. Their influence and the advantage of having received my education in a Catholic institution were what helped to plant the first seeds of my vocation to the priesthood.

Once in awhile the wild idea of becoming a priest would waft through my thoughts. Father Michael Mullner, the young, vibrant vocation director for the Bismarck Diocese, did everything he could to nurture that idea. I was fairly successful, however, in hiding behind my attraction to the opposite sex in order to counter any possibility for taking a lifelong promise of celibacy. Besides, I was already being fully indoctrinated by the "American Dream." I thought I knew what I wanted: lots of money, a position of prestige, and a beautiful wife and family with whom to share it all.

Following graduation from Trinity High School, I accepted a scholarship to the University of North Dakota. Upon arrival on the Grand Forks campus, I promptly joined a local fraternity and moved in before classes began. They say all roads lead to Rome, but it would have been difficult to imagine this one actually arriving there. In fact this road did take a quick detour.

A semester of this type of fraternal community was enough to satisfy my curiosity and I moved off-campus with a good high school friend of mine, David Fleck. By the end of the academic year, realizing that the lifestyle I was leading was doing nothing to satiate my desire for true fulfillment, I decided to give the seminary a try.

Next stop: St. John Vianney Seminary (on the campus of the University of St. Thomas in St. Paul, Minnesota). My time there really proved to be a mere hiatus in my further pursuit of the "American Dream." True, I was giving this priesthood thing a try, but at best, it was a half-hearted try. Still driven by my thirst for success, I was elected president of the seminary by the end of my first semester there.

Still entrenched by my need for attention, I never stopped dating. In fact, by the time spring arrived, I was involved in an exclusive relationship. That summer the rector of the seminary convinced me to return in the fall to finish off my term as president even with the understanding that I had no intention of breaking off this relationship. Two weeks into the 1989-90 school year I could no longer live with the charade. I resigned as president of the students, left the seminary and was convinced that I had given this wild idea of priesthood a fair try.

Three years later all of the elements of my "American Dream" were realigned in my prospects. As I prepared to graduate from the University of St. Thomas, I was engaged to be married (to a different women than the one I had been dating when I left the seminary) and

59

things were already falling in place for my entrance into law school: a prestigious position with the promise of money and a beautiful wife.

So what happened? Well, for lack of a better description, I think I hit the mid-life crisis a little early. You see, all the things that people told me were going to make me happy were now within my grasp and yet there remained an undeniable void. Not that there was anything intrinsically wrong with the goals I was striving towards, but I was seeking them with rather shallow, selfish intentions. I had set my heart on respect, esteem, and a steady source of affirmation. I expected my wife, my job and my money to satisfy the inner longing of my heart and it was becoming apparent that they might not be able to do that.

For anyone to place this kind of expectation on their family and occupation is the beginning of disaster. Only God can truly satisfy us. It was he who created us with the void so that we might turn to him for fulfillment. But nowhere within my equation of the "American Dream" was there any idea of knowing or serving God. I was serving myself, period!

Two months prior to our marriage, my fiancee and I broke off our engagement. Weeks later, I graduated with a degree in philosophy and had no idea as to what I could do with it now that my aspirations for entering law school had gone flat. This was really quite a low point in my life. But in the midst of a very confusing and trying time, a still, small voice continued to beat in my heart suggesting that there may yet be another path.

About a year prior to my engagement I had experienced a type of conversion. Once again, I was rooming with David Fleck, now in St. Paul, and one evening something possessed us to challenge each other to begin praying a daily rosary. The next morning we warily fumbled through the correct procedure of prayers marked off by this string of beads and it embarked us on a road we were both perhaps unaware even existed. Looking back, I have to believe that this "rosary-a-day promise" was Our Blessed Mother's foot stepping in the way of the slamming door of my soul. It invited me to taste the sweetness of prayer, of entering into intimacy with God. The impression his presence left on my heart kept me yearning for more and I actually began to entertain an idea of what it might mean to live a life pleasing to him. It was this taste of God that upheld me throughout a very painful, trying time of breaking off an engagement and questioning my whole path in life.

After graduation from college, I took a year off to sort out my life. I worked as a counselor in a juvenile delinquent treatment center. During this time I fell into contact with Father James Livingston and through his prudent, patient direction I was led to the decision of giving the seminary another try. I figured that I had already tested the roads I believed would lead to happiness. Why not give this idea of following God a real effort?

Prior to returning to the seminary, I first had to be accepted by a diocese who would sponsor my studies. This can sometimes be a difficult decision. Upon ordination I would make a promise of obedience to the Ordinary of this diocese (i.e. the bishop) and it is rare than an Ordinary would assign one of his priests outside of his diocese. So, in essence, the diocese for which you study as a seminarian is the diocese you will be serving as a priest for the rest of your life.

Despite having spent the past six years living in the St. Paul/Minneapolis Archdiocese, something drew me back to my home Diocese of Bismarck. Msgr. Gerald Walsh, the vocation director there at that time was quick to confirm this. I visited him in the spring of 1993 to discuss the possibility of entering the seminary. Our conversations resulted in acceptance by the Bismarck Diocese and September saw me departing for the North American College in Rome to study theology for the next four years.

Being in Rome was the break I needed from those who might have influenced me to further question this decision to follow Christ with my whole heart, mind and soul. I was able to give myself completely to the possibility of becoming a priest. By the grace of God I never seriously questioned this call again. Sure, there were periods of doubt, moments of yearning for an alternative lifestyle, but I think I realized that my personal efforts to create happiness were exhausted. I was content with following this new path which brought such peace and serenity to my heart.

Recounting the years of my seminary formation would surely require another chapter. God certainly continued his process of pruning this tree to prepare it for bearing fruit (as he does to this day). He placed an incredible supporting cast in my life throughout the process. He gave me men and women who challenged me to grow in holiness. I am especially thankful to my spiritual directors, Msgr. Daniel Thomas and Fr. Paul Murray, O.P., who supported, challenged and nurtured me every step of the way; to the communities of consecrated women religious whose enthusiasm, dedication and joy continue to edify me; to the men with whom I lived and studied with whose lives bear witness to the humanity and authenticity of our humble call, and to Sr. M. Patrick, M.C. and the religious Community of Missionaries of Charity to which she has given her life, whose example and encouragement strengthen me to this day in striving to offer with joy the price necessary to love the Lord my God with all my heart, mind and soul and to love my neighbor as myself.

I was ordained a priest on June 19, 1997, at the Cathedral of the Holy Spirit in Bismarck, where I now serve a parochial vicar. In the words of the Dominican priest, Lacordaire, *"What a wonderful life! And it is yours, O priest of Jesus Christ!"* What a wonderful life, indeed!

✣ EIGHT ✣

Father Roger Synek
As I Recall Him

When young Roger Synek first heard the words, "Whoever puts his hand to the plow but keeps looking back is unfit for the reign of God" (Lk 9:62), he was probably just a small boy on the farm and the words did not mean much to him. Roger grew up on a farm near Ray, North Dakota, and worked hard there as a boy and young man. He knew about plowing and harvesting. He knew about livestock and their needs. He liked the farm. He and his family worked hard together in that rural setting.

Roger graduated from high school and then enrolled at North Dakota State University in Fargo to study veterinary science. His dream was to become a veterinarian some day. He studied animal science in a pre-veterinarian program for two years and then spent two years as a vet technician.

Shortly after his graduation from college, Roger's father died suddenly at a very young age. Roger was the logical member of the family to return to the farm. With his agricultural education and his degree he thought that he was the ready to run the farm. Oh, there were moments when Roger felt the tug of God at his heart but he dismissed this as unimportant and gave his full attention to farming. Five years went by quickly and Roger discovered that the business of farming was a difficult venture. A lack of necessary moisture, along with low prices and great expenses made farming difficult.

As time went by, Roger's heart was not in the work he was doing. He slowly came to the conclusion that this was not the way he wished to spend the rest of his life. There was something more that attracted him. He began to pray earnestly to know what God wanted him to do.

It was at this point that Roger left the farm. He began to speak to certain people about a possible vocation to the priesthood. He was encouraged to continue to discern his calling but to take some time to do so. He returned to Fargo where he had attended college and worked in various types of employment. Using his agricultural education, he worked in a greenhouse for a year. This was not satisfying. He then found employment working in one of the parish rectories for a year. This brought him close to priests and also allowed him access to daily Mass and Holy Communion, spiritual direction and a regular confessor.

It was at this point that I met Roger for the first time. He had been in contact with the vocation office earlier and had been encouraged to take time to make his decision before applying for entrance to the seminary. When I met Roger he was not quite ready to make that application but he was getting closer. We met for lunch and I remember how impressed I was by Roger's openness and his blunt honesty as he shared the moments of his previous years and the struggles he had endured. We visited for some time and I remember Roger's closing remarks as we parted that day, with the promise to keep in touch. He said, "I don't know when I will be a priest but I know that I *will* be a priest, because I know that God wants me."

That fall Roger enrolled in the Vianney Program at Cardinal Muench Seminary in Fargo. This is a program which allows a young man to live at the seminary and participate in all of the seminary activities and program for one year without making a commitment. In that sense, he became sort of an "affiliate" with the diocese but not a registered or accepted seminarian. That was the year that Roger worked at the Olive Garden, a restaurant in the area, and became serious about his spiritual life.

It was a good year for Roger and at the end of the year he was ready to make application to the diocese for acceptance. He did so and was accepted to enter pre-theology that fall. Roger spent six years at the Pontifical College Josephinum studying theology and preparing himself spiritually and academically for ordination. They were not easy years. The demands of class work and study habits were difficult after being away from them for a number of years. The discipline required by the seminary was helpful but daunting at times. Through it all, Roger grew more deeply in love with Jesus Christ and his Blessed Mother. His prayer life flourished and became his source of great strength and stamina. They were years of dogged perseverence. The faculty and seminary officials were amazed and deeply impressed with Roger's determination and his forthright efforts. His accomplishments were inspiring. They were truly years of grace.

Roger is now a priest. He was ordained on May 27, 1998. The words of St. Luke are living words for Fr. Roger now. He had put his hand to the plow many years earlier, both in real life and in his spiritual life. As a young farmer he never looked back until the tug at his heart became so strong that he could no longer wait. That was when he put his hand to a new plow....to the work of Christ....and prepared himself diligently and graciously for that ministry. He never looked back over the rough and rugged roads which he had traveled. In his heart he knew what God wanted--for Roger to be a priest --and now was the time to do so.

Fr. Roger is a gentle and sensitive soul. He is gifted liturgically and his musical abilities have served him well as cantor, organist and liturgist in the seminary and continue to serve him just as well or even better in his parish ministry. His first year after ordination was spent at St. Anne Parish, Bismarck, where he served as parochial vicar–associate pastor. The fall of 1999 saw him named pastor of the Church of St. Martin at Center. He is well suited to serve a rural parish, knowing first-hand the struggles farmers and ranchers are currently facing. He will surely be a gentle and loving shepherd to his new parish.

He is loved and appreciated by all who know him, especially those whom he serves, and he continues to keep his "hand to the plow" with that constant effort and deep trust in God's love and grace which has brought him to this day. His story is the story of deep faith in the mystery of his vocation and of determined perseverance and trust in God's grace.

Father Roger's Story...In His Own Words....

I do not have many memories as a child of wanting to be a priest, but Mom recalled that I "played" priest once in a while. Throughout grade school, I memorized my prayers and learned my faith either through the Catholic school in Williston, or in CCD classes. During high school, we lived on a farm east of Williston and south of Ray. It became quite an effort to get to church. During the summer between my junior and senior year, I made a resolution to get back to church. By not attending Mass on Sunday, I realized something was missing. I decided that I would drive the 23 miles to town each Sunday and invite my other siblings along if they wanted to go. This was the beginning of my desire for God.

When I left for college, Dad gave me a Bible. I'd never read much from the Bible before so I decided that I would read a chapter a day. I did read the Bible from cover to cover twice. The college life was not really beneficial to my spiritual life. I would make it to Sunday Mass...most of the time. My focus was on getting "A's" in all my classes. My plan was to become a veterinarian, and the vet schools only accepted students with a 3.15 grade point average or above.

In January of my fifth year of college, my father died of a heart attack. As this was a crossroads, I had to make a decision--do I take over the farm or continue in school? I decided that I was needed on the farm. I would give myself five years to make a go of it. I then proceeded to farm--during five years of drought.

As I began those five years, I was mentally burned out from college. Adding five more years of anxiety and worry about how to get the bills paid didn't help much. In the fifth year of farming, I bottomed out. The motor on my tractor, that tilled about one thousand acres of farm land and fed about a hundred head of cattle, gave out. This was the straw that broke the camel's back. The cows were sold and the machinery auctioned off.

God was working with me through those five years. During the second year of farming, some of the people in our parish encouraged me to make a Cursillo. This experience lit a fire within my heart and gave me a desire to search diligently for Jesus. I began to pray the rosary and read the lives of the saints. In the next three years, I also attended a SEARCH weekend.

When I lost the farm, this ignited desire to search for Jesus brought me through it all. Not knowing what I was going to do with my life, I began to focus on discerning my vocation. All areas were open: marriage, priesthood religious life, or single life. Becoming a veterinarian was also still a possibility. So I went back to NDSU to finish the remaining two years. My focus was much different this time. I no longer tried for the "A's." Instead, I began to focus on listening to God and learning how to trust him. I was amazed how my grades drastically improved.

During the summers of these two years, I volunteered to work with the Sisters of St. Joseph in New Orleans. While there, I made a peaceful decision that I was not to become a veterinarian. I had never experienced such peace at making a "negative" decision before. I still remained in the animal science program at NDSU.

After graduation, I met with the vocation director of our diocese and discussed the possibility of priesthood with him and Bishop Kinney. We all agreed that I needed more discernment time. I lived at the Newman Center in Fargo at the time and to pay for my room there I worked at a greenhouse. Using the rhythm of the workday as a reminder to pray was a wonderful gift. I began to mentally pray all of the mysteries of the rosary. A few years later, I would discover that God was using this to teach me that the more I put "God thoughts" into my mind, the more they would crowd out other unwanted thoughts.

After some time, I met with Bishop Kinney again and we both decided that the time still was not right for me to enter the seminary. I needed more time to discern God's plan for me. In addition, we agreed that I should spend some time looking at personal issues such as dealing with an alcoholic parent. The experience of working as a rectory housekeeper and weekend janitor in a parish, as well as living in the rectory, revealed a clearer picture of a diocesan priest's lifestyle.

I had also been struggling with the celibacy issue for some time. Could I give up the intimate touch between a man and a woman in marriage? I read that celibacy must be seen as a gift, not as something one should "give up." I began praying for celibacy to be a gift in my life.

In January of that year, while kneeling in prayer, I opened the Bible to John 5:14. I read the words that Jesus said after he cured the man who had been sick for 38 years: "Remember, now, you have been cured." I was profoundly touched with these words. In that moment, I knew that God had touched me. The truth of his touch stood out above any doubts I may have had.

With this touch, I received the gift of celibacy in the form of an intellectual insight. As God touched me, I realized that I had been celibate for almost 30 years. If I was able to live a celibate life up until now, I certainly could live more years of celibacy. From this point on, I was free to choose among all vocational lifestyles.

After visiting with my vocation director and the bishop one more time, I realized that I still needed more time for discernment. I worked that year as a host and pasta maker in a local restaurant, and

I also entered the Vianney Program at Cardinal Muench Seminary in Fargo. As I discerned my vocation throughout that year, I found that the attraction of marriage slowly faded into the background while priesthood and religious life came to the forefront. By the end of the summer, my decision to enter the seminary remained. It was time to follow the "tug at my heart" and begin my seminary journey.

Seminary life at the Pontifical College Josephinum in Columbus, Ohio, would consist of six years--two years of philosophy in the pre-theology program, and four years of theology. Throughout the first year God gave me the gift of confidence in knowing that this was where he wanted me to be. This gift became the most convincing affirmation for me to become a priest as I experienced the daily pressures of a demanding schedule and academic struggles. I could see how God was strengthening my trust in him. All things worked out for the best.

In regards to religious life, I loved the chanting of the Psalms I had heard at our local Benedictine Abbey in Richardton and their life of prayer was very inviting. I would draw strength from their rhythm of prayer. Although I did not feel called to live the monastic life, I resolved that I would make time for this quiet prayer each day. This resolve remains with me today.

For the next four years God continued to reaffirm my vocation to the priesthood. On Saturday, June 20, 1997, Bishop Zipfel came to the Josephinum and ordained me and my classmates to the Diaconate. I was filled with joy. On My 28, 1998, he ordained me to the priesthood at the Cathedral of the Holy Spirit in Bismarck, and assigned me as parochial vicar to the Church of St. Anne, in Bismarck. I was named the pastor of the Church of St. Martin in Center in the fall of 1999.

What joy it has been to serve God as his instrument to sanctify his people here in the Bismarck Diocese. Each day is a joy. That confidence I received when he touched me in the rectory eight years ago still remains with me. I have learned, through my time spent in quiet prayer, that this is the Lord's presence in my life. I pray that each one of you who will read this story will find this steadfast presence of God in your life. When we do, life become joyful. When we listen carefully to this "Presence," we find our vocation. May you be blessed in your search as I have been.

NINE

Father Gary Benz
As I Recall Him

St. Mary's Parish in New England, North Dakota, is known for its large number of priestly and religious vocations. Over the years, this small parish has given a significant number of priests and sisters to the church. And so it was no surprise when word came to me at the vocation office that a young man by the name of Gary Lee Benz from New England was thinking of the priesthood. Gary had graduated from St. Mary's Catholic High School when I first heard of his inclination. In fact, he was already a student in college at North Dakota State University in Fargo when I contacted him and suggested that we meet.

It so happened that about that time I was planning a trip to Fargo and meeting Gary for lunch would fit well into my plans. I was new at vocation work and Gary was nervous about the possible commitment which a visit with the new vocation director might imply. We agreed to meet at the Catholic Newman Center on campus, where Gary was active in Peer Ministry. And so it was on a day in April of 1991 that Gary and I met for the first time.

Gary was not well acquainted with the campus as yet, nor with possible restaurants in that area. As it happened we ended up going to a neighboring "greasy spoon" for lunch just so that we could talk and get acquainted. We would often laugh about this later. The food was alright. The conversation was better. I soon learned that Gary was full of questions. He was eager to learn and wanted to know all about how one decides, how one knows if one should enter the seminary or not. Gary was studying history with the thought of becoming a secondary teacher after college. He was a good student in high school and continued his serious bent for knowledge and information in college. His curious mind served him well as he pursued every bit of fact and data he could find about vocations and priesthood.

We parted on that day with my promise of prayer for Gary and a promise from him that he would keep in touch and continue to pray and reflect on his possible call to priesthood. Over the next year Gary was good about communication. He felt the tug at his heart and yet he was not sure. Gary is the kind of man who needs evidence before making a decision. We all know that God does not always supply a lot of that to those whom he calls. Hence, a daily and oftentimes agonizing struggle took place in Gary's life over the next months.

During the next year, Gary continued his education toward a degree in history. All the while his heart continued to tell him that God had other plans for him. Being a real student, though, Gary decided to graduate with his degree in history and then begin his preparation for the priesthood. This was his plan but we will see that it did change during the course of the year. And it changed for the better.

Another struggle which Gary had during and after his decision to follow God's call to priesthood, was "to what form of priesthood is God calling me?" Was it the diocesan priesthood or the monastic priesthood in some religious community? Gary felt strongly attracted to each one. It was only after much prayer, advice, spiritual direction, and the weighing of the advantages and disadvantages, that Gary was finally able to come to the conclusion that it was as a diocesan priest that he would feel most comfortable. It was working as a priest in his home rural diocese where he felt God wanted him to be.

While this struggle was going on, in the spring of 1992, Gary also made the decision to enter the seminary program at Cardinal Muench

Seminary in Fargo, continue to pursue his degree in history, and also begin to take classes in philosophy and language which would help him later in the seminary. The good rector, Father James Ermer, agreed to allow Gary this chance and Gary was delighted. It was a difficult year of long hours of study and continued discernment, but in the end it was all worthwhile. The next year was easier. After two years there, Gary graduated with his degree in American history and also a degree in philosophy—obvious indications of what a good student Gary was and continues to be today.

The struggles of over two years seemed to be resolved as Gary began to think of theology and where he might best use his gifts and talents. The North American College in Rome was one of his choices and the bishop concurred. So it was that in September of 1995, Gary made his way to Rome where he studied for four years. Gary did well as a student at the Angelicum University in Rome, where he received a master's degree in ecumenism in the spring of 1999, in addition to a master's degree of divinity. He was ordained a deacon on June 24, 1998, and became a priest on the same day, The Feast of the Birth of John the Baptist, along with two of his classmates, in 1999.

This fine, young priest is a quiet, soft spoken man with a head full of knowledge and a ready wit. His quiet demeanor often belies the appealing sense of humor which lies just below the surface of his personality. He is highly respected by his peers, admired by faculty and students alike, and loved by those who know him best. His difficult struggles in the past have made him sensitive to those of others. Many will seek his advice and counsel in the years of his priestly ministry and Gary will be able to assist them.

Living and studying in Rome for four years, and being a true student of history, has given Gary a renewed love and respect for the past events in the church. It has been a love affair with time for him and his constant thirst for knowledge has served him well. His love for Christ and his church is apparent. Without being "bookish," Gary is able to share his knowledge and information in new and exciting ways. For the past four years, he was where God wanted him to be. That fact has given him the confidence that his entire future life will be determined in the same loving way.

Gary is from a large family of ten children. His devout parents have given each of their children a strong Catholic education and a deep understanding, love and respect for their Catholic faith. It is this strong German Catholic background which Gary brings to his priesthood. It has been a definite factor in his vocation and will endear him to the people of similar backgrounds whom he will serve in his priestly ministry. His academic interests will also serve him well as a possible teacher of high school religion in one of our Catholic schools as a young priest, and also as a parochial vicar in some parish, as well as a pastor at a later date. Gary Benz has much to offer to the church and he will be very generous in his giving, because, blessed with a grateful heart, Gary will always remember with great gratitude what God and the church has given to him.

Fr. Gary is currently serving as parochial vicar at the Church of St. Joseph in Williston.

Father Gary's Story....In His Own Words....

An interesting aspect of a priestly vocation is the uniqueness of this calling—every man has his own story of his journey to the priesthood. Some men experience the call to the priesthood after years in established and successful careers. Other experience the call in the midst of the soul-searching years of college, while others seem to have known from an early age that the priesthood was their vocation in life.

I fell into the last category. Already at a young age, I told my family and friends that I was going to be a priest. Such a bold proclamation was quite understandable, at least in my mind, because I was raised in an environment which was most supportive of priestly vocations.

I remember thumbing through my mother's, *A Mother's prayer Book,* which had a prayer card inserted in a section entitled "Prayers for Various Vocations." Among them were prayers for priestly vocations. As a young man, I was impressed by the pastoral zeal and joy of my parish pastors, especially in their sacramental and liturgical ministry. I was equally impressed by the zeal for Christ and his church evidenced in the lives of the School Sisters of Notre Dame who staffed St. Mary's, our parish school. St. Mary's has 14 priests and 18 sisters among its graduates.

With this supportive environment, I felt confident in responding to God's call to the priesthood and began making plans for seminary studies upon graduation from high school. But, in my senior year, things fell apart. I began to question my vocation. Perhaps I was too young? Perhaps things were moving too quickly? Should I go to college and continue to discern my vocation? Was God calling me to the Benedictines? And most unsettling, was I called to the priesthood? Rather than enter into seminary formation that fall, I enrolled in the history/education program at North Dakota State University in Fargo.

In hindsight, I was attempting to flee from God's calling, but he gently persisted. This calling grew stronger in my prayer life and was supported as well by the encouragement and personal witness of the priests at the NDSU Newman Center and the seminarians of Cardinal Muench Seminary, who enrolled in university courses at NDSU.

In time, God granted me the courage to once again answer his call to the priesthood. This call was now encouraged by the new vocation director, Msgr. Gerald Walsh, who offered needed guidance, wisdom and prayers. Upon completion of my history/education degree, as well as a year of discernment at Cardinal Muench Seminary (CMS), I entered the pre-theology program at CMS as a seminarian for the Diocese of Bismarck. It was a big step and not without the concerns of earlier years, but God provided me the grace to daily live what I daily prayed, "Thy will be done."

My time at CMS was filled with many graces, which contributed to a strengthening of my priestly vocation. My life became grounded in and sustained by the Holy Mass and the Liturgy of the Hours, the center of daily life at CMS. Blessed with a holy spiritual advisor and confessor, I became assured of God's infinite mercy and love and the mutual exchange of love in prayer–intimate conversation with God. At CMS, I also came to a more profound knowledge of God by means of the philosophical and classical studies at CMS. Indeed, CMS was a special place, especially with the fraternity among staff and seminarians who were united in the same goal to serve God and his church as holy priests.

At the request of my bishop, John F. Kinney, I continued my seminary studies in Rome. I entered into pastoral formation at the Pontifical North American College and into theological studies at the Pontifical University of Saint Thomas Aquinas, the Angelicum. Coming from peaceful rural North Dakota and being thrust into the business of Rome was quite an adjustment for the son of a farmer. It was an adjustment as well going from a seminary of 25 students to one of 175 seminarians!

With God's grace, I adjusted and the attributes which characterized life at CMS also characterized life at the NAC and the Angelicum. Yet, Rome offered special graces of its own: encounters with the Holy Father, Pope John Paul II, most importantly at papal liturgies; a rich spiritual heritage, especially the many tombs and monuments of the martyrs and saints; and a "Catholic" experience of the church, an experience of her universality, which is offered at the pontifical universities, which are comprised of students from all cultures and states in life. I will always treasure my brothers in Christ, the students at the Angelicum and the seminarians of the NAC.

On June 24, 1999, the Feast of Saint John the Baptist, I and two of my diocesan brothers were ordained priests of Jesus Christ for the Diocese of Bismarck. The awesome and sacred nature of this call is truly humbling. God personally chose *me* to serve as an instrument of his salvation in the person of Jesus Christ, his Son! I look forward to cooperating in this divine work of salvation, especially in the sacramental ministry of the church, and particularly the Holy Eucharist, the source of charity and unity in the church.

A priestly vocation is a gift from Jesus Christ offered through his church and I am eternally grateful for those faithful members of Christ's church whose many prayers on my behalf contributed to my perseverance in this sacred vocation. May God keep me faithful to my priestly vocation and may I and those to whom I minister join one day in the eternal hymn of praise offered to the Blessed Trinity in the glory of heaven!

I am now serving as assistant pastor at the Church of St. Joseph in Williston.

TEN

Father Bill Cosgrove
As I Recall Him

Tucson, Arizona, is a popular place for retired priests to seek some measure of comfort and relaxation in their senior years. Many migrate to this warm and sunny place because it promises a place where there is less pain from physical disabilities. Many also just want to avoid the harsh cold winters of the north. It was for this reason that Father John Peters, a priest of the Archdiocese of Dubuque in Iowa, found his way to Tucson to retire. Father Peters was well liked-- a beloved pastor and a dear friend to many. One of these friends was a man by the name of William Patrick Cosgrove. Bill is not a young man. In fact, he's a man who has seen a great deal of life, including heartache and suffering, and who welcomed the understanding and support of Father Peters.

Bill, like Father John Peters, was originally from Iowa. He had grown up there, attended a Catholic high school and had been faithful in the practice of his Catholic faith. When his friend, Father Peters, retired and moved to Arizona, Bill followed. He was anxious to be close to his priest friend so that he might help him, if needed, and care for him as he grew older. Bill took a job as a police officer at the Vet's Hospital in Tucson and it was thus that I first met him. But let's back up a bit.

As a young man, Bill had often thought of the priesthood as a possible vocation. The sisters who taught him saw something special in this devout young man and encouraged him to consider the priesthood as his calling. Alas, like so many young men who give serious consideration to this way of life in high school, after graduation Bill enlisted in the Air Force and was soon deeply engaged in the military. Thoughts of being a priest soon faded.

Soon after high school, Bill met and married a wonderful young woman with whom he intended to spend the rest of his life. They became the parents of two little girls and life was good. Soon, however, it became more and more evident that his wife was beset with emotional problems which made it difficult, indeed impossible, for her to take care of her marriage and her family. These problems soon became so severe that she had to be hospitalized and Bill became a single parent. Eventually a divorce took place and Bill continued to raise his daughters with the help of his family.

Finding it too difficult to be both father and mother to his two little daughters, Bill decided to take a different direction. Of course, annulments were scarce in those days and so Bill entered a civil marriage with another single parent and together they raised their five children. As the years went by and the children grew up, Bill felt the void in his life which the absence of the sacraments created. He and his partner decided to separate and a civil divorce followed so that Bill might return to the active practice of his Catholic faith.

Years went by and Bill sought employment in various business ventures. Some of these involved travel and he spent a lot of time on the road. When annulments became possible and more available in the church, Bill applied and the annulment was granted.

During this time, Father John Peters became a very good friend of Bill's and one day he asked Bill if he ever thought of becoming a priest. Father John's priest friends also encouraged Bill to think about a vocation and so the seed was planted once again and the idea began to grow.

Because of his age, Bill did not give it serious consideration at first. He was now in his middle 50's and life was passing him by. He prayed for guidance and to know God's will for him at this point in his life. Finally, he decided to give it a try and began to write letters to a number of dioceses to see if any of them might accept him. The negative replies were a great disappointment to Bill and also to Father Peters, but Father was not about to give up.

It was January of 1994 and I was visiting in Tucson, Arizona, for a few weeks. Earlier, through a priest classmate of mine by the name of Father Tom O'Flannigan, I had met Father John Peters and we had become friends. One day in January, during the course of my visit, Father Tom and Father John and I went out to lunch. We decided on a little German restaurant on Broadway called the Kuchen Dutch. In the course of our conversation, Father Peters started to tell the story of his friend, Bill Cosgrove, who was looking for a diocese to accept him. At first the story just seemed like ordinary casual conversation, and then it occurred to me that he was making a plea to me as vocation director to consider Bill for our diocese.

In the publication entitled, *Program for Priestly Formation*, No. 595-x, Fourth Edition, November 1992, from the National Conference of Catholic Bishops, on page 98 paragraph 522, it states, "A number of candidates at the time of their initial application to the seminary are older than in the past. Many of these applicants have completed college and often some years of work in areas other than theological education or pastoral ministry. Bringing a rich and varied background to the seminary, they represent an asset to the seminary program and to the community." As you will read in their stories, a number of our seminarians were "older" men. Bill was older still. As Father John and I visited, I became more and more interested in the fascinating story which Father was telling. Finally, I told him that, while I could make no promises before visiting with my bishop, I would be happy to meet Bill and visit with him while I was in Tucson and then I could better decide what to do.

Bill must have been praying very hard. Of course, it helps to have several good friends who are priests and who are interested in helping you. At any rate, before the afternoon was over, Bill and I met and spent some time together. From the outset, I was sincerely impressed by this man who had lived quite a life and was now ready to begin a new one. I tried to ask all of the right questions and Bill's answers gave me courage and hope. It was an inspiring discussion and I could see that Bill was, indeed, ready for the seminary if he could only find a bishop to accept him.

I went home and began the process of application with Bill. Our bishop was willing to give him a chance. We completed the application process and on May 19, 1994, Bill Cosgrove drove with Father John Peters all the way to North Dakota to be interviewed by Bishop John F. Kinney, the current Ordinary.

The bishop was as impressed as I was. Bill's "moment of grace" had come and he had responded with all his heart. The journey had begun. It was only a matter of time before Bill was accepted in the seminary and began his five year preparation for priesthood. Bill's age has never been an obstacle. He is young at heart and filled with zeal and energy for the Lord. He has lived and worked in several of our parishes during the years of his theology studies, and our priests have been singularly impressed by his love of Christ and the church. His willingness to be of assistance in any situation is a tremendous example to our younger men. Nothing is too difficult for Bill to undertake. He is generous to a fault and couldn't wait to be ordained a priest so that he could begin using all of his talents and gifts for God's people.

Bill Cosgrove heard the invitation of the Lord to leave it all behind and follow him. Bill has not been disappointed. The years of study and spiritual formation have not been without some hardship and difficulty. This is understandable for one who was away from the books for 40 years. Nevertheless, Bill has been outstanding in his dedication and determination. He felt the tug at his heart as a young

81

man. With marriage, family and work intervening, it took some years for that tug to be felt again. Now it is so strong that Bill's whole life is filled with the desire to be what God wants him to be and to do what God wants him to do. He will be a most effective and successful priest.

To his priestly ministry he brings a wealth of experience and a host of gifts and talents. He is a caring and loving person who understands the difficulties of married people, older people and also young people. He has lived a life of many experiences and all of that will enrich his priesthood and endear him to everyone. We pray that he will have a long and blessed life and many, many fruitful years of priestly service.

William Patrick Cosgrove was ordained a deacon on June 24, 1998, and a priest on the same date just one year later. This past June, for Bill, was the fulfillment of Jesus' invitation, "Come follow me and I will make you a fisher of men." Fr. Bill Cosgrove, at age 63, is ready.

Fr. Bill is presently assigned as parochial vicar at our Catholic Indian Mission at Fort Yates, North Dakota, where he continues to work with those who have less of this world's goods but are rich in faith.

Father Bill's Story....In His Own Words....

Being born in 1935 in our neighborhood was to be a part of the Great Depression. We were all in the same circumstances of poverty. There was a certain amount of security in knowing that all of your neighbors knew from experience the situation of each other. People that had anything at all seemed to share what extra they had, and those of us who had little were happy to be on the receiving end of food or clothing. These early circumstances of life had a lasting and profound effect on me in later years in terms of being able to understand better the plight of the down and out. I thank God that the experience was no worse than it was for our family, but I thank him also for the experience and how it helped to shape my life.

We were a family of nine. I have three brothers and three sisters and we all get along very well and are very close to each other for the most part. We had to depend on each other for a lot of our companionship, especially at play, and we looked to other relatives for outside social contacts. We could only afford family get-togethers with our aunts and uncles and cousins, which made us a close-knit family. As I look back, I had a very happy childhood.

I can recall starting school and bringing a rug for naps and a box of color crayons. This school thing seemed alright to me because we got a carton of milk right away and a lunch later on--and then a nap. Many of my classmates from St. Patrick's School in Cedar Rapids, Iowa, and I went through the thirteen grades together and we still gather with spouses once each August. From the very beginning I liked school.

My dad was a good man who worked very hard as a laborer, truck driver or welder, as the opportunity arose. He seldom missed work and we always had a roof over our heads and some food, even if it was only toast and hot tea. I don't recall when it happened, but Dad, Joseph Patrick, started drinking. He would periodically do "binge drinking" and would be mean to Mom and occasionally to us kids. My three brothers and I seemed to be less affected by this than were our three sisters. I think, to some extent, they carried psychological scars from it for quite a long time. In the end, however, Dad spent his retirement years, as well as a few years prior to retirement, as a loving father and grandfather.

Mom was the saint and the solid timber that held the family in place during hard times. I always remember her being at home, and yet I know she worked as a telephone operator and a hotel switchboard operator. She must have worked the late shift to bring in some money, yet she was always there for us kids during the day. Mom baked what we called "johnny cakes" or maybe a pie. I recall that with nine of us in the family, and the pie cut in only eight pieces, Mom was never hungry for dessert, so she said!

During our school years, we went to Mass as a class quite often, at least once a week and at times, more often. I do not remember ever going to church as a family. I enjoyed being at church with all of the students, and I did not understand why some did not like it. Some said they felt forced to go, and I never felt that way. The Sisters of Charity taught us that Jesus Christ was present in the Eucharist, Body and Blood, Soul and Divinity, truly present. I have never doubted that fact even for one minute of my life. It is this belief that kept me from every doubting the teachings of the church

Because of my Catholic education and faith, I always felt a sense of worth, of confidence in myself. My mother and the sisters and the good priests that we knew growing up always made me feel good about myself. Keeping in mind the time, I had what I felt was an average childhood with many blessings and few disappointments. I was never picked first for playground activities and sports, but I was always picked early in the choosing. I always felt badly for those with lesser abilities in sports who were always chosen last. I was always confident of the school lessons and here again, I did not excel but I felt confident.

Because I was the older brother, I got to be the priest when we played church. This was probably the earliest I recall of being interested in the priesthood–at about the age of six or eight. I would wrap a dish towel around my neck and be "Father" and have Mass. When we tired of church, the same towel could be my Superman cape as I jumped from high places

It was in the eighth grade that sister made me an altar server and, again, I thought about the priesthood. Learning the Latin was very difficult but being up there with the priest was worth the effort. It greatly increased the value of the liturgy for me to see Father's face and the love and care with which he handled the Sacred Body and Blood of Jesus Christ.

I was really glad to graduate from high school and I worked in a corner gas station that summer until September. I had talked to the Armed Forces recruiter and decided to join the Air Force. I had a hard time breaking the news at home, but I did it and, after a few tears, my decision was respected by all. My youngest brother was only seven and it was hard to leave Dave. I knew that he would hardly know me later.

The Air Force was a great adventure for me. After we passed the physical exams in Des Moines, Iowa, we were soon on a train for boot camp in Syracuse, New York. Here I was just seventeen, almost eighteen, and seeing America.

After boot training, which was fairly uneventful except for the good food (the best food I ever had), I was headed across America. Stopping for nine days in Cedar Rapids for a visit with family and friends, I then returned to the Greyhound bus and finished the trip to technical school in Hayward, California. The school was for Air Base Defense and I was destined to be an Air Force policeman.

I completed Air Police School and was allowed a 30-day leave back in Iowa before returning to California to be shipped to Japan for two years. Wow! This was quite a bit of traveling in less than a year for an eighteen-year-old. I enjoyed every minute of it, but I did miss everyone at home.

It was during this time of my Service career--and that was my decision that it would be my career--that I realized how truly fortunate I was. I really did have a great education, thanks to the sisters. All of the testing I had to do in the first year showed me the advantage that I had over guys from other parts of the country. Even the one semester typing course came in handy. I had a desk sergeant's job that kept me warm and dry working inside most of the time. I was very happy and settling in to enjoy my career.

I returned to the states and while enjoying another 30-day leave before going to my new base in Fort Worth, Texas, I began dating a girl I knew from our school days. We went to different schools but knew each other fairly well. We had many good times together during those 30 days and it was difficult for me to leave for Texas. We kept in touch as much as we could and decided that we should get married in the summer of 1956. That August we had a small wedding at the Carswell Air Force Base Chapel. Now I not only had a career in the Air Force, I also had a vocation as a husband. The only problem Shirley and I thought we had was money. It was hard trying to live on Air Force pay. However, this was not our only problem as we soon discovered.

Two children were born to this marriage: Linda Kay in 1958 and Joy Therese in 1962. After the birth of Linda, it was apparent that my wife, Shirley, was having mental problems and these became more and more serious as time went on.

Soon it was necessary for Shirley to be hospitalized and undergo a series of terrible shock treatments during the 1960s. The prognosis was that Shirley would not be able to carry out the responsibilities of marriage and family life, but she would be able to manage her own life and care for herself, which she did with the aid of family. So for all practical purposes our marriage ended and we were separated, with the exception of a two week reunion on one occasion, and an attempt to live with our children as a family. This attempt was not successful and I returned to Cedar Rapids with our two children. I received a "hardship" discharge from the Air Force and in 1971 I obtained a civil divorce.

In 1971 I entered a civil marriage with Janice Henderson who had three children from a previous marriage. At that time annulments were not common. We joined our two families and this blended family endured for thirteen years. Janice was a wonderful mother and later a grandmother. The children were raised very well. I missed the practice of my faith, however, so in December of 1984 we separated and a divorce was granted.

Sometime in 1984 I met Father John Peters, who at that time was the pastor of St. Mary's Parish in Vinton, Iowa. We became very close friends and traveled together on several occasions. In 1985 I accompanied him to one of his class reunions and it was at that event that several of his priest classmates began the discussion about the possibility of the priesthood for me. They agreed that there was no reason why I could not be reconciled with the church and receive the sacraments again. In fact, that very day, I received the sacrament of reconciliation in the parking lot of a truck stop.

Since then a steady growth has taken place in my love and thanksgiving to the Lord, those two priests, Father John Peters and Msgr. Billy Roach, and the church. Msgr. Roach was going to assist me in the annulment procedure but his life was cut short by an auto accident. Since then Father Peters, my mentor, benefactor and best friend, helped me discern my life and future. On one occasion he pointed out an article in a paper or magazine telling of an older second career vocation person who had been ordained a priest. From that time on, my hopes and dreams were to focus on that goal.

I began the annulment process with the help of Father Peters and after three years of waiting, it was granted by the Tribunal of the Diocese of Tucson. In the meantime, I worked as a police officer at the V.A. Hospital in Tucson and in Iowa City, Iowa. I began to prepare for the necessary academics by attending classes in religious studies at the University of Arizona, taught by Father Robert Burns, Ph.D., O.P. In 1992 I made a pilgrimage to the Holy Land.

I began to make application to various dioceses for acceptance as a seminarian. Many bishops do not accept older men and so the response was disappointing. In January of 1994 I met Msgr. Gerald Walsh, the vocation director for the Diocese of Bismarck, and he agreed to speak to Bishop Kinney about me. I was happy to hear from him that Bishop Kinney was willing to consider me and that he wanted to meet me. In May of that year, Father John Peters and I drove from Tucson to Bismarck to meet Bishop Kinney. The meeting went well and I was accepted. September found me at Sacred Heart

School of Theology in Hales Corners, Wisconsin, a seminary for older men. I was on my way toward my goal of the priesthood.

In 1997 my dear friend, Father John Peters, went home to God. He would have loved to see me ordained but his work was done and he is with us in other ways. I will always remember his kindness to me and the encouragement he gave me when the future did not look very bright. His family gave me his personal chalice and I shall think of him and pray for him each time I celebrate the Eucharist with this precious gift.

The five years at Hales Corners were not the easiest years of my life. It was difficult to return to classroom studies after being away for so long. Several illnesses caused me some concern, but with the grace of God I was able to complete my studies and formation program and be ordained on June 24, 1999. Only God knows how many years I have left to serve him and his people, but I know that I will do my best to give all that I have to my priestly ministry. With the help of God I will be a good and holy priest for the years that God gives me.

ELEVEN

Father Keith Streifel
As I Recall Him

For many years the people of our diocese have been praying a vocation prayer which was composed, printed and distributed throughout the diocese by one of our former bishops. It is a good prayer and popular in our parishes. Subsequent bishops have continued to distribute copies of the prayer and encourage its use. Obviously, as grace works, this prayer has quietly touched the hearts of many young people and given them the support they need to respond to God's call.

The prayer begins like this, "O Dearest Jesus, Son of the Eternal Father and Mary Immaculate, grant to our young people the generosity necessary to follow your call and the courage required to overcome all obstacles to their vocation....." All obstacles to their vocation. A large order, indeed. Realistically, we all know of the many serious obstacles our young people face in their lives today. We also know that some are never able to overcome all of them and never make it to the seminary or religious community.

Some, however, give their vocations a try, enter the seminary or convent, and then after a time they decide that this is not for them and they return to their former life. Most of these folks will never try it again.....a few will discover after some time that they really are being called by God to be a priest or religious and will return, at last to the place where they really belong.

So it was with Keith Streifel, a bright and very personable young man who grew up in one of our larger parishes–St. Joseph Parish, Williston--and graduated from the local public high school. Whether it was entirely the deep faith of his family, his grandparents and parents who were, and are, devout Catholics, or whether it was the priests he came to know, or whatever, Keith came to know and love Jesus Christ and the church. He was a faithful altar boy and knew his prayers well. At any rate, and Keith will tell you more in his story, during his high school years he became involved in Search and some other spiritual teenage activities and liked what he had found. He was faithful during those years and, at time, felt a real tug at his heart to consider the priesthood as his vocation.

He met Father Michael Mullner, one of our popular young priests, who was vocation director at that time. Fr. Michael encouraged Keith to think about the seminary, and so he did. The tug was not strong enough at the time, however, so Keith enrolled at Michigan State University, declaring chemistry his major. He soon learned, though, that this was really not his first love and so he switched his major to philosophy, which would allow him to be with and work with people. Keith is a people person and loves to interact with others.

At any rate, it was not long before Keith was being drawn closer and closer to a decision by God's grace. The moment of decision had come and Keith responded by applying to the diocese for acceptance as a seminarian and enrolling in St. John Vianney Seminary in St. Paul, Minnesota, to complete his college work.

".....Grant to our young people the generosity necessary to follow your call and the courage required to OVERCOME ALL OBSTACLES to their vocation." Keith did very well in the seminary, but when graduation came in the spring of 1989, Keith decided that he was not ready for theology. There was something that told him to wait and so he left the seminary and his formation for priesthood at that time.

Always a very outgoing and very sociable person, Keith felt drawn to seeking some employment which would provide contacts with young people and where he could share his faith with them and support them in theirs. He was hired as a youth director in a parish where he enjoyed the work and found satisfaction in his ministry to young people. Soon he realized, however, that his ministry could reach beyond parish lines and The National Evangelization Team (NET) seemed the right place for this to happen. Keith became involved in their spiritual work of evangelizing young people throughout our country, particularly the Midwest.

Keith gave his total energy to this work. His heart was really in it. He loved what he was doing and he did it very well. His musical ability, voice and instrumental, served him well in his new ministry and he touched the hearts and souls of a multitude of teenagers, sharing his faith and inspiring them in theirs. He moved up in positions as a member of NET and became one of the leaders in that special organization. All the while, though, as happy as he was and as satisfying as his work was, Keith realized more and more that there was something missing. He could do only so much for these young people in spiritual ways. As a priest he could do much more.

Finally, in June of 1995, Keith came to see me about returning to the seminary. It was our first meeting and I was deeply impressed by his sincerity and his humble awareness of God's grace and goodness. Keith had traveled a long and sometimes very difficult road and his journey was not an easy one. Nevertheless, it had now brought him back to where he had found happiness some years ago and this is what he was looking for again. Had the obstacles disappeared? Were the prayers of the people of our diocese for that intention successful and effective for Keith? Prayer is a powerful force. We stand in awe of its power.

This bright, intelligent young man returned to the seminary that year and completed his theology at the North American College in Rome in the spring of 1999. He learned Italian with a flare because his classes were taught in that language. He loved Rome and all of its richness. He was very much at home in Italy and became comfortable with Italian food and drink. He honed his culinary talents so that he can prepare wonderful Italian meals for his friends. He enjoys social events and communicates well.

Keith Streifel was ordained a deacon on October 8, 1998, in the Basilica of St. Peter in Rome, along with his classmates at the North American College. He was ordained to the priesthood on June 24, 1999, at the Cathedral of the Holy Spirit in Bismarck. The journey for Keith has taken a number of years–interrupted years–years of faith and ministry and, at last, years of final decision and grace. Keith will continue to serve the young people of the church in our diocese with great love and care as he has in the past. Now that he is a priest for and with them, he will be able to do even more for their spiritual lives. He will touch their souls as never before. Keith Streifel has come home and his family and the church of Bismarck rejoice.

Fr. Keith is now working at St. Leo's Parish in Minot as parochial vicar and teaching high school religion at Bishop Ryan High School, the local Catholic high school. His love of young people is just as strong as ever.

Father Keith's Story...In His Own Words....

Over the years I have described my journey to the priesthood in many ways. All of them are true but each of them highlight different aspects of the many ways that God has worked in my life to bring me to where I am today. Much of the movement of the Spirit in my life has been of the deep, quiet kind--a sort of a tug on the sleeve inviting me to "Come and See!" So much has this been true that I used to say that God never struck me with a two-by-four, some sign which I couldn't deny and which would move me absolutely in one way or another. On the other hand, as I look at the strength of some of these tugs and all the instances of God's invitation, I recognize a landscape littered with lumber.

I cannot say when I first felt the tug of the heart. Perhaps this is precisely because I grew up in the environment of faith that I did, where not only was devotion simply taken as a given but where I saw the example of my parents striving to grow in faith and love of Jesus Christ. My first recollection is in grade school. A priest asked, "Have you ever thought about being a priest?" "I'm thinking about it." I replied.

"I'm thinking about it," was my response throughout high school and even into college, when Fr. Michael Mullner invited me to visit a seminary with him. I must have been thinking about it enough that I didn't surprise many people when I told them I would be going to that seminary a year later. Even for me, as I took the decision to prayer on a retreat, the choice to enter the college seminary seemed obvious.

During this time there were a few things that continued to stand out in my memory as urging me onward. The first was simply the presence of Fr. Michael, whose obvious love for God and the priesthood spurred him, even in the midst of a losing battle with cancer. He would say, with absolute joy and confidence, "God is good." He was a witness to be argued with for the Christian life and the priesthood.

The second was a visit with Bishop Kinney who said, "One of the things I love about being a priest is that when I walk into a room, people expect me to talk about what's most important to them--God and the things of God!" Many times I have heard stories of Bishop Kinney saying that he couldn't imagine doing anything else.

I loved my time in the Saint John Vianney Seminary in St. Paul. I was able to continue to "think about it" but I was also pushed to go deeper and to really consider many aspects of ministry in the church.

I had to start to choose, and "I'm thinking about it" was only the first half of the sentence. The rest, "....if I don't get married," I usually left off. I began to understand that eventually one of the phrases would have to be pruned for the thing to grow. The problem with my second phrase was not so much that it was an option, in fact it became decisive in my returning to the Diocese of Bismarck, but that marriage seemed to me a cure-all thought. "If I were to find the perfect woman, my life would also become perfect, and since God wants the best for me...Q.E.D...".

I really began to understand that I believed this argument only as it was time to graduate from the College of St. Thomas where the seminarians took their classes. As attractive as the seminary and priesthood continued to be for me, I could not go on to the major seminary with such doubts.

I left after college to work in a parish as a youth director. My youth minister in high school had helped me so much to grow in faith and understanding of the church that I always wanted to try to help others experience the same.

I also tried real dating for the first time in my life. I was challenged with two realizations. My syllogism, or what had passed for one, was false, and I was not the youth director I wanted to be. I found that relationships were not the elixir I had imagined. Rather, like the rest of life, it could be a mixture of joys and woes. In working in the parish, I found that I wanted a stronger theological background to deal with all of the complexities of life and that I sought a broader ministry than youth, though that continues to be one of the most energizing things for me. Then I was accepted as a member on a youth-retreat team for the National Evangelization Teams. I was attracted to NET when they came to the parish where I worked. Their vibrant and energetic prayer was something I wanted to experience.

During the three years I traveled with NET, I saw many healthy families, lived through the ups and downs of our team "family" and found myself very attracted to a much more realistic notion of marriage and family life. At the same time, I saw many healthy priests who ministered to me, and continued to grow in desire to serve God in the priesthood. I loved NET but in my heart of hearts I knew that God had another plan for me. Still, every time I tried to pursue the priesthood, I felt like a dog who had reached the end of its leash.

For the most part, this was a purely internal phenomenon, but one which was confirmed in discussions with my supervisor, and later with my spiritual director. I tried dating. No, that's not entirely accurate. I looked around for someone to date. I met many holy, wonderful women and made some great friends, but I couldn't bear to bring them into my indecision. I reached another "leash-end."

I tried to look for an order or a religious community, which I thought might be a good synthesis of my two attractions. Wherever I turned I found closed doors (in one case, literally) or communities which weren't what I was looking for. I have since seen many communities which seem to me to be what I was looking for at the time, but at the time God put none of these in my path. I eventually got the hint. I had long wanted to be a missionary, so I tried to pursue that for the time being. However, all of the organizations that were taking volunteers wanted either more money than I had--since I was already volunteering--or more time than I was willing to give (two to three years).

Somehow I felt that the Lord was calling me to give my all, to give myself away generously in his service, and I knew of only two ways to do that for me: marriage or the priesthood. I am oversimplifying perhaps more than a bit. Everything I've already mentioned was swimming around in the soup of decision, but in the end that was the way the question made sense to me. In fact, I was trying to decide whether to take a job teaching religion or to stay with NET another year when this became clear.

A number of people has told me that they were glad they didn't have to make the difficult choice between two good positions: my roommate, my supervisor, my parents, and another person who had applied for the teaching position. In other words, none of them were any help.

So I went out for a long run, weighing the pros and cons of the options before me and praying for clarity. As I neared the end of the run, God answered my prayer. There was no voice, no neon sign, but as if God was running right along with me, I understood, "Look, I can bless you whether you do this or that. Sure, I have my preference...but I want you to choose." I also understood that this was not only for my job choice, but it meant that I needed to decide for the priesthood since I knew that to be my choice. When I think about it now, I am honored and awed by how much God respected my free will, even when I wished he would have just told me what to do. I am also amazed at how well the Lord knows me. I think about how often I have done things without really choosing to do them, and doing them sloppily and half heartedly.

That's the punch line of the story. It looks good on paper, but I'm still working it out. It took another year and considerable prayer inspiration by the Holy Spirit to get me to call Msgr. Walsh. Even then, I had to warn him that I thought I was called to an order, and therefore I might jump ship at any moment....if only the right ship would float by. Monsignor was most understanding, "I think that is a good place to be, why don't you come in so we can talk some more?"

In the seminary I continued to deepen and develop that choice. The Lord continued to teach me that my choice was not only for a way of life, or even a vocation understood as a religious way of live, but a choice for a person, the Person of Jesus Christ. I, like all Christians, was to be conformed to him, but more particularly conformed to him through my priesthood. I was also very concerned that my choice not be mine alone, but that it be God's choice.

I was blessed last fall to hear, in the Rite of Ordination of Deacons, "We choose this man, our brother, for the Order of Deacons." I heard the same, "we choose this man" at my ordination to the priesthood this past summer (1999). Nowhere else do I know of the church so directly confirming a calling. Perhaps not everyone hears those words as powerfully as I did, because we know that Jesus says, "You have not chosen me, I have chosen you." But the loving Father knew that I needed to hear them, just as he knew that I needed to hear, "You must choose."

✛ TWELVE ✛

Deacon Daniel Berg and Deacon Christopher Kadrmas As I Recall Them

It was the spring of 1992. On an April weekend, our diocesan vocation team sponsored a "live-in weekend" at the local Benedictine Priory. The weekend consisted of Friday evening and all day Saturday. Five people responded to our invitation--two women and three men. All were strangers to each other and to most of us on the Team.

We spent the evening and following day reviewing the meaning of "Vocation," reflecting on God's ways of calling, and emphasizing and experiencing prayer. When the weekend was over I invited the three men to my office to further explore their interests and spiritual journeys. The three men were as different as their backgrounds. Two of them had grown up on farms, and one of them was the son of a school teacher. The three were from points in the diocese and the state which were a hundred or more miles from each other. They had little in common except that they all felt a tug at their hearts and knew that they could not be at peace until they dealt with that unrest. Finally, after weeks, months and, in two cases, years of discernment, all three of these men entered the seminary. As fate would have, they all ended up in the same class and, God willing, all three will be ordained priests together in May 2000.

The following story is an account of two of those young men. One of the three chose not to be included in this story. We all respect his decision.

My Memories of Deacon Dan....

To that weekend in April of 1992 came a young man who grew up on the land. His parents owned and operated a farm near one of our small rural towns. Dan had grown up on the farm and loved it. He attended college after high school and had earned a degree in accounting. For a number of years he had been employed as the bookkeeper of a small Catholic hospital near his home. Dan loved his work and the sisters loved Dan's work as well. Dan loved the farm but knew that this was not to be his future work. He was and is a very meticulous person, deeply conscientious and somewhat of a perfectionist. All of these good traits served him well in his accounting work but became a stumbling block in his discernment process about his future.

Dan wondered about that future. Did he want to continue in accounting for the rest of his life? Did he feel fulfilled in what he was doing? Dan was older--30 years old in 1992-- to be exact, and yet he was unsettled. He felt a strong attraction to the priesthood and had been encouraged by many people, and yet, being a shy person, he agonized over what the priesthood would demand of him and how he might publicly live that life day by day.

Dan and I would meet several times over the next two years. Each time we would review how God was working in his life and each time I would encourage Dan to give the seminary a try. All the while Dan was growing in his faith and his prayer life. His attendance at daily Mass was an important part of his day and the tug at his heart was growing stronger. Many questions were asked and many answers were given. Slowly the voice of God grew stronger.

Finally, two years later, in June of 1994, Dan began to prepare to enter the seminary. Since he had his college degree it would not be necessary for him to begin college all over again. He would enter what we call "pre-theology" and study philosophy for two years in preparation for theology. Dan's two years of prayer and discernment were over and he had, at last, surrendered to the Call.

Like Frank, the third man at the "Discernment Weekend," Dan is now in his fourth year of theology and will be ordained with Frank and Chris in less than one year, God willing. His deeply conscientious approach to life and to God's people will make Dan a very caring and sensitive priest. He has been an inspiration to everyone and will serve well as confessor and spiritual director to many souls. Dan Berg's decision was not an easy one, but his "moment of grace" came through and the journey goes on.

Deacon Dan's Story... in His Own Words...

My name is Dan Berg. I am currently studying at Kenrick School Theology in St. Louis, Missouri. I was ordained a transitional deacon on May 2, 1999, and am now in my fourth year of theology. God willing, I will be ordained a priest in May of 2000. I am 36 years old and considered a "later" vocation. I am the second oldest in my class of 15 at Kenrick Seminary.

I grew up on a farm near Max, North Dakota. My parents are Doris and Clifford Berg. I have two younger sister, Deloris and Dorothy. The call to the priesthood takes me back to my grade school years at Max Public School. When I was in the second grade, our teacher, Mrs. Lee, asked us what we would like to do in our lives after we graduated. I wrote on the little round slip of colored construction paper that I would like to become a priest. Each of our little circles were then pinned to the bulletin board. Well, I guess that struck some of my fellow students, especially the guys, as being a little strange, for in the years to come they began to tease me about this action of mine. Some of them called me "Father Berg." I really despised that at the time. This teasing went on through high school. I was a shy and introverted student and, as a result, this teasing hurt me all the more.

Looking back, I could see God's grace working within me in other ways. I really enjoyed going to Mass. I had a longing in my heart to be like the priest who was in our church. I would even take some missalettes home and play Mass with my sister or other friends who came to visit. Even though this seemed pretty crazy, I can see now that somehow I was cooperating with God's grace.

When I was a high school senior and had to make that big "career choice," I really did not know what to do with my future. I had feelings about wanting to study to be a priest, but yet I did not want to be teased about it. My favorite subjects were math and accounting, so I made up my mind to work toward an accounting degree. Our Lord would not let me go at that point. He seemed to be ever pulling me toward him in his love. He also works in humorous ways.

I graduated from Max Public School in 1980, and was accepted into the accounting program at Mary College (now the University of Mary) in Bismarck in the fall of 1980. I enjoyed school very much, but was not interested in speech or even taking English. For some reason, I decided to take a foreign language--French. How could I ever come to think that this was easier than English? It was a challenge to speak and write in French. My French teacher, Sister Helen Kilzer, OSB, was a very challenging professor. I eventually took four years of French which replaced all of my English courses.

I soon began to realize that a foreign language helped me to understand Latin and Greek--two languages that I took later at Cardinal Muench Seminary. The highlight of taking French was going to France in the spring of 1982 during the month of May. Three other students and I, plus the professor, Sister Helen Kilzer, (our guide), went as a class. We visited many churches throughout France and England and one of the main highlights was the shrine at Lourdes.

I graduated from Mary College in the spring of 1984 with an accounting degree and business and French minors. I lived at home on the farm with my parents for the next ten years, helping them farm. At that time my dad had some medical problems, so many of the farming responsibilities fell into my arms. During that summer, I applied for a job as a computer trainee at a bank in Garrison, a neighboring town. It was mainly an evening job which lasted from about four o'clock in the afternoon to about nine o'clock or midnight depending on the day of the month. Even though this job was kind of boring, I felt that it was an excellent opportunity to have a job and still help my parents on the farm during the daytime. Sometimes I got time off to help with the harvest in the evenings.

This job lasted about 2 ½ years. I had been looking for a different job during this time, but this particular job was very convenient since Garrison was only 12 miles from our farm. Eventually, I came across another combined job opening in Garrison at the Garrison Memorial Hospital and the Garrison Ambulance District. The bookkeeper's husband was being transferred to another location, so she had to give up her position. I applied for the job and was hired within a few days.

This job proved to be the opposite of the previous one. Whereas the work at the bank was boring, this one was almost too much for me. It seemed like there was too much work and too little time to do it. I enjoyed the work, even though I struggled with it. I felt that I should continue with it since it was so close to home and I could still help Dad farm.

During this time thoughts of being a priest returned to me, but the thoughts were a little stronger now. I had developed some good Catholic friendships at the hospital, and I tried to pray the rosary most every noon in the hospital chapel after lunch. Our Lord gave me the grace to do good work at the hospital and kept me sane during the time I was struggling.

The Garrison Memorial Hospital was owned and operated by the Sisters of St. Benedict from Annunciation Priory in Bismarck. I developed some good friendships with Sr. Bernice, Sr. Madonna, Sr. Camille, Sr. Moira, Sr. Francis, Sr. Rose, and others. In the spring of 1992, Sr. Camille Jorda encouraged me to attend a discernment weekend at the Priory in Bismarck. At first I was unsure of this but I decided to give it a try. This was a "live in" weekend in April, sponsored by the diocesan vocation team. It consisted of a Friday evening and Saturday. This team discussed the possibility of a vocation with us. There were two other men and two women there who were complete strangers to me. The other two men, Frank Schuster and Chris Kadrmas, also eventually entered the seminary and are currently in the same diocesan class of the year 2000 as I.

Along with Sister Camille on the "team" was Monsignor Gerald Walsh, the diocesan vocation director. After that weekend, a variety of things changed in my life. A Knights of Columbus member asked me if I wanted to join the Garrison K. of C. Council. I joined in the summer of 1992 and almost immediately became the program director. About that same time, our pastor in Max, Father Jerome Schommer (now deceased) , asked for older men to volunteer to serve at Mass in the Max Parish, because there were not many Mass servers in the parish. This was before girls were allowed to serve at Mass. After much thought, I decided to help out.

It all seemed to happen so fast. Through participation in the Diocesan Discernment Weekend, my involvement with the Knight of Columbus, my becoming an active Mass server, and through the encouragement of many family members, friends and relatives, I decided to give the seminary a try in the fall of 1994. God's call for me to serve him in this special way kept getting stronger and stronger for me and I felt that I should do something about it before I got too much older. It was at this point in my life that I entered Cardinal Muench Seminary in Fargo, North Dakota, to begin my seminary formation.

Going back to school after being away from it for ten years has not been easy for me. Philosophy was difficult at times and also the writing of many papers, but there is an interior happiness within me that comes from following God's will and not running away with mine. It is a very different life not earning money for a living, having no steady income and trusting that others will provide for my needs in various ways. It is a sacrifice for me not to be working on the farm and in the healthcare industry as I enjoyed that work very much, but I feel that God is calling me to a life of service to others as his priest. I do not know what the future holds for me, but I trust in the way that the Holy Spirit is leading me and that is all that matters..

* * * * *

My memories of Deacon Chris....

Another man at the weekend in April of 1992 was Chris Kadrmas from Bowman. I had known Chris for two or three years prior to this time. I met Chris at a SEARCH weekend and was impressed with his questions and his interest. Being the son of school teachers, Chris was the typical "student," very curious about knowledge and always thirsting for more. Chris had been chosen to be part of a program called Peer Ministry while at the university where he was studying social sciences with the thought of working with children with behavioral problems. The program of Peer Ministry kept Chris close to the Lord through shared prayer and mutual ministry to his classmates through the local Newman Chapel. It was there that Chris seriously began to ponder his future and where God was leading him.

It was also there that Chris met a special young woman and fell in love. Thinking that marriage was his vocation, he became engaged and began to plan for that vocation in life. In his own story, Chris will tell of how he came to decide differently as God's grace began to grow stronger and the tug at his heart became more and more real.

Chris was chosen for this special Peer Ministry in this secular university because of his obvious deep faith and his pursuit of virtue. It was a great privilege and honor to be chosen and Chris rose to the challenge, as always, and was a very successful minister to his peers. It was a good indication of the Lord's special interest in Chris, and a possible future vocation. It had Chris wondering and praying but he was not quite ready. And yet, he did come to the 1992 weekend and he asked all of the right questions.

Again, being dedicated to knowledge and education, after the 1992 weekend, Chris decided that he would put off making a decision until he had graduated and worked for a year or two. In 1993, Chris had graduated and was working at a local Catholic hospital in occupational therapy. Chris loved his work and was very good at it. He received many references of appreciation for his expertise and could have made an honorable career in this field. He exercised obvious gifts and talents in leadership roles during this time and his ministry to others was done with great care and sensitivity. Chris was a "minister" in the real sense of the term but not quite ready.

All the while, however, the tug at his heart continued. We met at every opportunity and also corresponded regularly during those months and two years. Chris had found a good spiritual director in one of the local pastors, and was being drawn deeper and deeper into the mystery of his vocation. Always the student and always curious for more information, the final decision to enter the seminary did not come easily for Chris. Daily prayer and a lot of support from other seminarians and priests made the difference.

In the early spring of 1994, Chris informed me that he was ready. We immediately began to prepare for his entrance to the seminary in pre-theology, and that fall Chris joined Frank and Dan in their seminary journeys. Like them, he will be ordained in less than a year and the three men who came from different places, different backgrounds and different experiences of life finally came together in one purpose, one calling, one hope and one dream. Even now, Frank, Dan and Chris are all studying in different seminaries but are all in the same class of theology.

It is all part of the great mystery of a kind and gracious God who provides for his people in very different and exciting ways. Chris continues his sincere formation, his search for truth in knowledge and his pursuit of virtue. He will be an outstanding priest and leader of God's people.

Deacon Chris' Story... In His Own Words...

I never really thought seriously of a vocation to the priesthood until a priest challenged me. I was actively attending our busy Newman Center/Catholic Parish during my college years. The local pastor was a priest who seemed to love what he was doing, and he was very good at his ministry as well. This intrigued me and I began to see priesthood as potentially fulfilling. This pastor also challenged many young attendees of the Center to consider vocations to religious life and ordained ministry. I was one of them.

I was most interested, however, in getting a degree and a job and, most importantly, in getting married. I was often drawn to the Newman Center because there I found many young people who had the same questions and values about life that I did. I met many women who were great marriage material. But during this time I was also thinking more and more of exploring a vocation to the priesthood.

I eventually was asked to be part of the Newman Center staff as a peer minister, one of the many students who helped introduce new campus students to the parish. I became more serious about my faith and about the church. Yet my desire to find a mate remained.

For me the vocations to marriage and priesthood seemed to be competing and at odds! Nevertheless, I moved forward in one special relationship with a young woman despite the nagging question of priesthood. We soon became engaged to be married. I thought that I could convince God of my choice to be married, and then he would leave me alone. Yet this was not so.

During the engagement, I often prayed that God would bless my growing relationship with my fiancee. Yet, in prayer, all I could hear was a silent, yet profound voice at the core of my soul saying, "This is not who you are. This is not who you were meant to be." I knew I could run no longer. My fiancee and I called off our engagement and I resolved to take my discernment further. I would have to go to the seminary.

Many of the priests I knew, including the pastor at the Newman Center, encouraged me not to move to the seminary immediately. They encouraged me to get a degree and work for a while as I continued to discern my vocation. It was at this time that I attended various SEARCH weekends as well as "live-in" weekends for vocations. I began a dialogue with Monsignor Walsh and he was very supportive of my own timetable for discernment.

I finished my degree in occupational therapy and worked for nearly two years at a small Catholic hospital in North Dakota. I worked with all kinds of people, most of whom were hospitalized for depression and other mental health conditions. I greatly enjoyed my work and my single life. All the while I was still discerning and came to the conclusion that God and the church were still calling me to ordained ministry. It seemed that despite the fulfilling work I was doing, there was something more that priesthood could provide people that therapy could not. I was also strongly supported by many local pastors in my on-going discernment. I soon contacted Monsignor Walsh with my intention to start the application process for my home diocese of Bismarck.

Since being accepted by the Diocese of Bismarck, I have completed nearly five years of seminary life at the Pontifical College Josephinum in Columbus, Ohio. In the spring of 1999, I was ordained as a transitional deacon. In the spring of the year 2000, six of us men hope for ordination to the priesthood for the people of the diocese. I have been graced abundantly by God through this mysterious journey of discernment. I will not ignore the fact of many ups and downs throughout these many years, but I continue to be thankful for God's generous plan for me in this world and for his church.

Left to right: Keith Streifel, Gary Benz, Msgr. Walsh, Tom Richter, and Wayne Sattler.

The North American College crowd...

Msgr. Walsh with his first two seminarians, Patrick Schumacher and Austin Vetter.

Left to right: Keith Streifel, Gary Benz, Chris Kadrmas and Frank Schuster serve as acolytes at ordination.

Dan Berg receives the Book of Gospels at his ordination as a transitional deacon. Serving as acolyte is another seminarian for the diocese, James Link.

Msgr. Walsh gathers at the 1999 Fall Clergy Conference with some of his seminarians who are now ordained clergy for the Diocese of Bismarck. Back row, left to right: Fathers Patrick Schumacher, Tom Richter, Keith Streifel, Austin Vetter, Bill Cosgrove and John Mathai. Front row: Father Roger Synek, Msgr. Walsh, and Father Wayne Sattler. Not pictured: Fathers Leonard Savelkoul and Gary Benz.

Bishop Zipfel presides at the transitional deacon ordination of Gary Benz and Bill Cosgrove. Acolyte is Mike Kautzman. At right is Father Patrick Schumacher, pastor of the Church of St. Mary, New England.

Serrans are great supporters of vocations. Here several members of the Minot Serra Club pose for a picture with, left to right: Father Wayne Sattler, Terry Wipf, Gary Benz, David Richter, Chris Kadrmas, and Msgr. Walsh.

Father Roger Synek at his First Mass in Williston.

Vocation director Msgr. Walsh pays a visit to the seminarians at the Pontifical College Josephinum in Columbus, Ohio. Left to right: Fred Harvey, Roger Synek, Msgr. Walsh, Chris Kadrmas, Terry Wipf, and John Mathai.

The Hales Corners students Leonard Savelkoul and Bill Cosgrove, both now ordained priests for the Diocese of Bismarck.

Seminarians, left to right, Chad Gion, James Link and Chris Kuhn enjoy a game of cards with Jerry Richter and Father Ken Phillips.

Left to right: Jim Shea, Shannon Lucht and Frank Schuster.

Left to right: Fred Harvey, Peter Eberle, Paul Eberle, Mike Kautzman and Chad Gion.

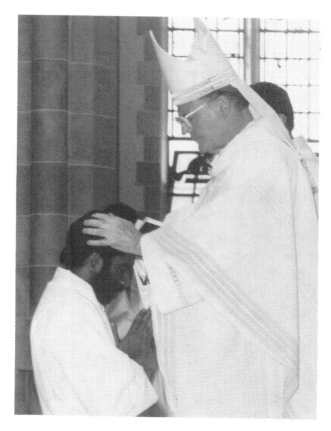

John Mathai at his transitional deacon ordination.

Summer fun at Msgr.'s cabin at Lake Tschida!

THIRTEEN

Deacon Fred Harvey As I Recall Him

In the life of a vocation director, there are many moments of frustration–moments which demand a great deal of patience, prayer and the wisdom to say the right words at the right time. Even then, dealing with the vocations of some men takes weeks, months and even years before they have the "moment of grace" which enables them to say "yes" to God's call.

Others are so easy that you wonder how it all happened so quickly. Often a lot of basic ground work has been done already when the candidate comes and so things move along quickly.

This is how it was with Fred Harvey. The phone in the vocation office rang one afternoon and the caller was a Benedictine sister from the local monastery. Sister Denise Ressler, OSB, had called to tell me of a friend and former student of hers who had indicated in a phone conversation with her that he was thinking of the seminary.

At this time the young man, Fred Harvey, was living in Tucson, Arizona, and was employed in Federal Law Enforcement as a Deputy United States Marshal. I had never met the young man but I told Sister Denise that I was planning a short vacation trip to Tucson and would be happy to visit with Fred about this. I asked for his phone number; it was given and I placed a call to Fred immediately. He answered. We visited briefly and I told him that I would call him when I arrived in Tucson and we would meet. He seemed happy about this.

It was November of 1993 when I was again in Tucson. Fred and I agreed by phone to have lunch at Applebee's on Broadway. It was a prophetic meeting and I sensed that Fred was perfectly at ease in discussing his interest in a vocation to the priesthood. His background was that he had been born, raised and educated in Bismarck. His family still lived there and his father was the sheriff of Burleigh County. Fred's family had been in law enforcement for some generations, but now he was beginning to think about a different future–a future in the church as a priest. He felt that God was calling him to a life of service in another way, and he was ready to get on with it.

Fred had lived and worked in Tucson for a few years, had become acquainted with some of the priests there, and had shared his thoughts about priesthood with some of them. They, of course, were anxious for him to join the local diocese and work with them. It was timely and providential that my contact was made when it was. Otherwise, Fred may now be preparing for a priestly life in the south rather than in his own home diocese. God does work in strange and mysterious ways. His family is happy that he is "back home."

Fred was ready to begin the application process. I was impressed by his prayer life and his mature approach to the matter of a life-long commitment to obedience and celibacy as a priest. We began the process and I left an application form with him when I left to return home after my brief vacation. Within the month, Fred's completed application arrived in my office. He was that ready. He had made his decision. He had responded to the "moment of grace" and his journey had begun.

In January of the next year, I made another trip to Tucson to review Fred's application with him, and to get to know him better. Again, I was impressed by his mature approach to life and his vocation. Fred was approaching 30 years old at the time and was anxious to begin his preparation, both academically and spiritually, for priesthood. By May, the month of his 30th birthday, Fred had given his employer his notice of resignation. He had sold his house in Tucson and had made arrangements to move back home to Bismarck. When he arrived in Bismarck, he met with Bishop Kinney and was officially accepted as a seminarian for our diocese. He entered the seminary in pre-theology in the fall of 1994.

Fred has shown continued maturity, good judgment and common sense in his prayer life and his seminary formation. He has been recognized by his peers for those virtues and was elected by his classmate as a representative on the Student Council the first years of his time there. He has also been chosen by them to be their representative on the Corporate Board of the seminary. He continues to do well in his academic and spiritual activities. Fred is anxious to be a priest and he will be a very good one. The rector and staff at the seminary recognize his gifts and have invited him to serve in various capacities during the years that he has been there. Fred has served generously and with great charity, constantly concerned for others and their needs and always willing to do more.

In the spring of 1999, Fred was ordained a deacon, along with the rest of his class, and next May, in the Jubilee Year of 2000, Fred will be ordained a priest with five other classmates for the Diocese of Bismarck. It will truly be a Jubilee year for them and for all of us.

Deacon Fred's Story.....In His Own Words...

I was born, raised and educated in North Dakota. Most of this time I lived in Bismarck with my family. After graduating from Minot State University with a degree in criminal justice, I applied for a job with the Department of Justice U.S. Marshal Service. I was interviewed, tested, and began working for them in early 1986. I was stationed in Denver, Colorado, and Tucson, Arizona.

After eight and one half years of working for this agency, I became more and more aware that, in some way, I felt that my life was not complete. It was while I was living in the Denver area that this awareness began. Not knowing what it was that was missing I continued to explore life and decided to try living in a place completely foreign to me. That is when I moved to Tucson and began working there. I knew no one and had no relatives in the area. It was a complete break from everyone and everything and a new beginning for me. Six months later, I decided that I liked it very much in Tucson and I decided to buy a house there. And so a three bedroom home with ample living space, a fireplace, and a swimming pool in the backyard, was mine, or at least I was paying for it.

All seemed to be going well and then I looked into becoming a registered member of a parish for the first time in my life. The parish I found was about a mile away from my home. I had been attending Mass in this parish even before I bought my house and moved into it. I liked the parish and the priests and people there and so it wasn't long before I began to feel that I should become more involved in the community and social life of the parish. The Life Teen program was looking for core members to lead the meetings and be with the high school teens of our parish. I inquired about the group and made a commitment to help out. They understood that my job and my work might take me away from home from time to time. This was acceptable to them and so a new wave of friendships began. Something new and exciting was happening to me.

The parish was assigned a new associate pastor. He was a former school teacher and approximately my age. Father Rudy and I became close friends and spent time together talking, playing golf and going to movies. What I found most interesting about this stage in my life was that even though I was tired from working all day, I would still go to the parish to be with the teens and share their activities, and afterwards find myself full of more energy than when I first arrived. In my prayer, those days, I would find that this was speaking to me.

One evening I decided to discuss this matter with Father Rudy over dinner. The conclusion was that maybe I was being called to service as a priest. Now I had some serious thinking to do.

A few months later, I drove home to Bismarck for a vacation and a family reunion. I was dating a nice girl at the time, but that relationship seemed to be strained as I was having so many other thoughts. During my travels I found plenty of time to talk with the Lord and during my return trip I had come to the conclusion that I was going to make a day of recollection, which was being sponsored by the Diocese of Tucson.

Upon my return to Tucson and my job, I discovered that there were numerous problems developing within my work environment. I finally asked to be reassigned back to general operations and to train a new person for the job which I had held for a couple of years. Being relieved of that heavy burden also placed me in a better position to seriously look at the possibility of leaving the job completely.

I attended daily Mass at the cathedral just a block or so from work, praying for an answer. I also attended the day of recollection and met with the vocation director for lunch a few days later. One day I was asked by the associate pastor if I had given any thought to being a priest in my home diocese. To be honest, the thought had never crossed my mind. I liked Tucson and just presumed that my vocation was to that diocese.

After thinking about this possibility, I called Sister Denise Ressler, OSB, a Benedictine sister who is a friend of mine in Bismarck, and asked her for the name of the vocation director there. Needless to say, she was very excited about all of this and said that she would find out and have him call me. I made her promise not to discuss this with anyone at the time. The next day at work I received a call from Msgr. Walsh, the vocation director in Bismarck. It turned out that he was planning a trip to Tucson in a couple of weeks and so we planned to meet then.

When Msgr. Walsh came to Tucson that November, we met a couple of times to discuss my possible vocation to the priesthood and my future with the Diocese of Bismarck. He was very helpful and I found in him a person who truly loves the priesthood, just the example that I needed at that moment. Before he returned to Bismarck, he left an application package with me and I began to fill out the paperwork. The completed forms were soon in the mail to Msgr. Walsh and I awaited his next move.

In the meantime, I had to start thinking about selling my house and determine when I would resign from my job. Suddenly, this all seemed too much for me and I began to think that I was making a mistake. I finally told a good friend of mine what was going on. He was very supportive and gave me much encouragement. I then told the people with whom I was working at the parish, including the associate pastor, that I had decided to go to the seminary to find out where God wanted me, and that I would most likely be studying for my home diocese. Although they really did not want me to go back to Bismarck, they were very happy for me and they also gave me much support in this decision.

In November of 1993, after spending a weekend at a youth rally, I made a telephone call home to inform my parents of my decision. Both were very accepting and encouraging. Though I had no details for them, I told them I would let them know more very soon. That year I decided not to travel home for Christmas and my parents came to visit me instead. We spent the week between Christmas and New Years Day together.

February of 1994 arrived and I had to make a decision as to if and when I was going to follow through with this. After speaking with Msgr. Walsh some more about everything, I got the courage to call the realtor about my house. The difficult part of this decision was that the diocese had not yet officially accepted me and so I was taking steps to quit my job, sell my house and move to Bismarck, without knowing anything for certain.

My trust was now totally with whatever the Lord was going to do with me.

At this same time, my name was among the top three individuals recommended for the supervisor's job in the Bismarck marshal's office, my home town. I guess either way, I was headed back to Bismarck. Now it was March and my trust in the Lord overwhelmed me. The house was sold within a week. A "for sale" sign was never placed on the property. It all happened so fast. The same day I received word that a friend of mine had been given the job in the Bismarck office. That settled that question.

Closing on the house was scheduled for the second week in May. Now I needed to let people at work know what was going on. I confided in just a few friends at work about my plans but decided not to give anymore than a month's notice. So I waited. April came and I gave notice to my superiors at work that my last day of employment would be May 15th. This was not well received, but from then on everything happened very quickly.

My oldest sister, her husband and family, were all moving back to Bismarck about three weeks ahead of me. I contacted her and asked if she needed any household furniture and the like. She said of course, but that it would cost too much to move my stuff back to Bismarck. I decided to rent a moving truck and take most of my household belongings back with me so that they could use whatever they wished. Everything I had was fairly new and hardly used so I felt that it was going to be put to good use. My roommate at the time, a friend who had shared the house, helped drive the van to Bismarck with my own vehicle in tow.

I was home again and it was very good to be there. The day after arriving in Bismarck I met with the bishop and was officially accepted as a candidate for the priesthood, a seminarian, for the diocese. It was a great feeling!

For the rest of the summer, I sort of "re-grouped" and took time to clear my head from the past eight and a half years of working in law enforcement. I spent a great deal of time at my parents' lake property and meeting a number of other Bismarck seminarians. The bonding between these guys and myself came about very quickly and I soon felt very comfortable with them. That fall four other seminarians and I loaded our vehicles and headed for Columbus, Ohio, to the Pontifical College Josephinum, a place I had never seen before but only read about. I had decided, with the consent and approval of the bishop and the vocation director, to take my pre-theology studies at a major seminary so that I might experience life in that type of a community from the beginning of my seminary formation. I have not regretted that decision.

It's now more than five years later and in just a few months, God willing, I will be ordained a priest for the Diocese of Bismarck and begin my life in priestly service to God's people. The time has gone by very quickly. It is with great joy and happiness that I accept my vocation and believe that God has called me to this life. I am grateful that he also gave me the grace and courage to respond. Many people have played an important role in this process with their prayer, support and encouragement along the way. It is to all of them that I say "thank you," and I look forward to serving them in the years ahead.

To any of you who may read this, I say, "Maybe, by the grace of God, my story may help you to answer the call to serve God in a special way, as a priest, sister, brother or deacon." This is my prayer.

FOURTEEN

Deacon David Richter
As I Recall Him

In the Gospel of John we read the story of two sets of brothers, James and John and Peter and Andrew. The Sacred Scripture is not clear about the sequence of which brother or brothers answered the call of Christ first. We do read in that same Gospel as follows, "One of the two who had followed him after hearing John was Simon Peter's brother, Andrew. The first thing he did was seek out his brother and tell him, 'We have found the Messiah. He brought him to Jesus....'" (Jn 1:40-42)

In the wonderful Richter family of Victor and Mary, there are 10 boys and 4 girls. I have described this good Catholic family in the story of their other son, Father Tom Richter, who is now a young priest. I mention Father Tom because I am not certain whether it was Father Tom who brought David to Christ, or David who, like Andrew, brought his older brother to Christ. At any rate, it is not unusual for two brothers to "follow Christ" and become priests. David is still in formation but in less than a year he will join his brother, Father Tom, in pastoring souls in priestly ministry.

Who is David Richter? I first heard of David as a possible "vocation" when he was still in high school. Through my friendship and contacts with the Richter family, I knew that it would only be a matter of time before one or more of the 10 boys would enter seminary. Perhaps this presumption on my part and on the part of many others put some unpleasant pressure upon David. At any rate, he kept toying with the idea of priesthood but also kept it at arms length, sort of in the back of his mind. He decided to wait and see. David is deliberate in what he does.

David, like most of his brothers, was strong and athletic. Smaller than some of his older brothers, David was built more like his father. Nevertheless, his strength in wrestling was well known and in his senior year in high school he, too, became a state champion wrestler. David was a good student--bright and intelligent, not afraid to ask questions and always looking and searching for the truth. He was particularly interested in his Catholic religion and wanted to know more about his faith. He dated and enjoyed the company of young women, always looking for signs that this was to be his vocation. He was never certain, however, that this was for him.

I met David when he was a junior in high school. We were both members of a pilgrimage to Medjugorje and we shared some special moments on that journey. David suffered from diabetes and we prayed for a healing on that trip. He was ready and open but also willing to accept whatever God would bring him. His diabetes is still part of his life, but perhaps it was his vocation which was strengthened on that pilgrimage instead. He has learned to live with his diabetes--as well as his sacred calling.

David returned to high school and, although we did not keep close contact, I did stay interested in David and his future. We met several times after that and visited briefly about his vocation. Uncertain as he was, David decided to study engineering in college and he was happy in his choice.

In the meantime, his brother, Tom, had entered the seminary and was happy there. David was drawn to seminary life but did not want to appear to be following so closely in his brother's footsteps. People might misinterpret his decision.

If and when he would enter the seminary, he wanted it to be strictly his own choice, and not influenced by big brother, Tom.

In 1992, David and I corresponded and visited about his future. He was still working on his degree but was interested in entering the Vianney Program at the seminary where he could live and pray for a year with no formal commitment. We agreed that this was a good thing to do. He could have the advantage of living a good solid spiritual life along with the seminarians while discerning his future. It was a good year for Dave. He was able to live and share his faith openly. His presence there was a great influence on our other seminarians and Dave himself was greatly influenced by them. It was a win-win situation.

As the year drew on, David became more and more convinced that this is where God wanted him to be. The "moment of grace" had come and he had responded. On October 18, 1993, David and I met to discuss his application for the seminary. He was ready to begin "the journey." He would become a seminarian in the fall.

He was in the college seminary for two years, catching up on languages and philosophy and preparing for theology. They were years not without some doubt and question. At seminarian gatherings, David often spoke freely of his lack of complete conviction about his vocation. A virtuous and dedicated young man, he wondered openly about celibacy and how one lives it for a lifetime. He thought of his parents and their wonderful large family. He remembered the good times that he and his brothers and sisters had experienced while growing up. He was attracted to that way of life, to that vocation. And yet, his heart told him that God was calling him to a larger family....the family of God, and he would be "Father" to all of God's people.

David graduated with a degree in industrial engineering and a degree in philosophy. He was ready for theology. Prayer, sincere and humble, brought him through. Trusting in God's grace and his love of the Eucharist, David persevered through the college seminary and

119

is now in his fourth year of theology. He was ordained a deacon in the spring of 1999 and will be ordained a priest in May of 2000.

He is a happy seminarian, content in his response to Christ's call. He has "found the Messiah," and left everything else behind to follow him.

Davis is a born leader. He is respected and admired by his peers. They listen to him when he speaks. He is fearless in the open practice of his faith. He does not hesitate to offer good insights to questions and behavior patterns of others. He enjoys a good time and recreates with the same enthusiasm as he prays.

Different from his priest brother in many ways and yet both strong leaders, they share a common zeal and love for Christ and his church. Like James and John, and Peter and Andrew, they will serve devoutly and be willing to suffer for what they believe. Theirs will be a positive and joyful ministry, and, who knows, perhaps through them many others will be called to "Come and See.....we have found the Messiah."

Deacon David's Story...In His Own Words....

I am David Richter, the sixth son and eighth child of fourteen children (ten boys, four girls) of Victor and Mary Richter. I grew up on a dairy farm 18 miles southeast of Bismarck, North Dakota. My father attended Crosier Seminary for five years, I believe, before discerning that God was calling him to the vocation of marriage.

Through his experience at the seminary, my father developed great friendships. He still maintains these friendships and keeps in contact with priest friends and those who left the seminary to marry. My mother attended a Catholic boarding school at Richardton, North Dakota. Her family has always been very religious. She had three uncles who became Benedictine priests and three aunts who became sisters in the same religious order. Thus, I was always in contact with those who had been called to religious vocations and was comfortable with that possibility for myself.

I remember, as a child, when my family would travel to Crosier Seminary in Minnesota for Dad's seminary reunions. It was then that I began to think of becoming a priest. But, like many thoughts of childhood days, it did not last long before something else would take its place, like playing basketball, football or billiards.

I was a trusting child and became deeply hurt if anyone tried to have a laugh at my expense. I still recall some of those instances and it has been part of my personal growth to let go of them and forgive those who took part. This has been essential for me to learn to trust others and also trust God more deeply and have the grace to answer his call.

Growing up in my large family and needing to protect my self interest, I learned to be very competitive and independent. I was quite athletic and a good student. In the fourth grade I became very ill and ended up in the hospital. I was diagnosed with diabetes. It slowed me down for a while but I was not going to let this condition wreck my life so I faced it head on and was determined that I would not be labeled as "different." There were a few times in my life when this proved to be a poor idea and resulted in some humbling episodes of insulin shock. All in all, however, I managed pretty well to live a normal life and even won the state class "A" wrestling championship in the 145-pound weight class in my senior year in high school.

I dated girls in high school and enjoyed partying with my friends. but during that time I also thought about my future. What should I do? I truly believed that it would be a good idea for me to check out the seminary like my father had done. I felt that it would be a good way for me to find out what God wanted me to do. But not yet! I wanted to go to college and study engineering first. So in the fall of 1989 I began my college work in pre-engineering at Bismarck State College.

I enjoyed college and I liked the engineering field that I was studying. I lived and worked at home during my first two years of college. At the end of my first year my brother, Tom, told me that he was going to enter the seminary. I was happy for him but at the same time it made my decision a bit more uncertain. You see, I did not want to be overshadowed by Tom. There was a part of me that was pleased that he was entering the seminary first. He could sort of pave the way and discover the difficulties so that I could avoid them later.

There was another part of me--that old independent streak--that wanted to be the one to make the big decision on my own without any direct influence from Tom or anyone else. During this time, Tom and I sort of drifted apart. Maybe it was because he was in the seminary and following a new path and I wasn't. Maybe it was because I needed to separate myself from his vocation in order to be more free to make my own decision. At any rate, on one occasion, he and I got into a heated argument and I felt hurt by some of the things he said to me. It took me back to the early years of my life, being hurt and misunderstood, and so I decided then not to trust anyone, not to share my struggles because I did not want to be vulnerable.

After two years of college in Bismarck, I transferred to NDSU in Fargo in the fall of 1991 to study industrial engineering. At the end of the year, Tom finished philosophy and I was hired for a six month internship at Polaris LP Company in Roseau, Minnesota, as a student engineer. I was helping to manufacture snowmobiles and all terrain vehicles. That summer at Polaris was a good experience and at the same time a difficult one.

At the time I was dating a beautiful girl who was the oldest of a family of thirteen children who lived on a dairy farm in Minnesota. We had a lot in common. I was working in my field of study which I enjoyed, but I had committed myself to give the seminary an honest look. At the end of the summer I returned to Fargo, and my decision still was not clear.

I learned of a new program at Cardinal Muench Seminary, Fargo, which allowed a person to live at the seminary with no commitment, and work or attend classes at the local university. It was a way to test one's vocation. I decided to enter the Vianney Program, as it is called, and so in January of 1993, I began to live at the seminary. It was like being a seminarian in action but not in name. I knew that I wanted to go to the seminary to allow God to show me where he wanted me to be. I hoped that after one semester or one year I would find that he didn't want me at the seminary and then I could continue to date the same girl and possibly marry.

You see, this was what I had planned, all nice and neat, but that was not God's plan. I felt the struggle of wills, mine against his, and it made my time at the seminary onerous because I wasn't really giving myself to the program. I was just trying to validate my own desires. In the spring of 1994, I graduated with a bachelor of science degree in industrial engineering. During that summer, I decided to officially enter Cardinal Muench Seminary in Fargo and was accepted as a seminarian for that fall.

The following spring I made a vow that if I found an engineering job I would take some time off from the seminary to work. To make a long story short, I never found an industrial engineering job and by the end of the summer I knew that I wanted to return to the seminary.

My evaluations at the seminary were quite good even though I was still struggling with accepting God's call for me. In the spring of 1996, I completed the pre-theology program at Cardinal Muench Seminary and graduated with minor degrees in philosophy and accounting. It was time to move on to theology, time for another major decision.

At the time the Diocese of Bismarck was without a bishop. Msgr. Walsh, our vocation director, was also the administrator of the diocese. He and I had some serious discussions that summer about my future. I was considering the possibility of taking a year off from seminary studies but was also struggling with an attraction to Kenrick

Seminary in St. Louis for theology. No other seminarian from our diocese had ever studied at Kenrick. Would I be allowed to study there? Msgr. Walsh convinced me that taking a year off was not the best choice for me at that time. He encouraged me to continue my seminary studies and was willing to allow me to attend Kenrick Seminary, at least for one year to see where God would lead me from there. The grace of God does wonderful things and that decision has proven to be been one of the great blessings of my life.

I have now been at Kenrick Seminary for three years and they have not been without questions and wonders about answering God's call in my life. At the same time, the past three years have been a time of growing certitude in my response to God's call. I credit much of this to the great faculty and staff at the seminary, who give their time and effort to assist men like me to discern how God is calling us to serve his church. Talking with friends, classmates and spiritual directors has been a source of great strength and support for me. They have helped me find and work through the obstacles which have held me back from fulling answering God's call with all my heart.

I cannot say that I will be the best preacher or the best liturgist but I pray that I may be a holy priest, a priest with integrity. I am most thankful to God for calling me to holy orders as a deacon on May 2, 1999, and I am grateful to all of the wonderful people who have supported me in so many ways over the years, especially by their prayers.

I am certain that God is calling many other men and women to serve him in priestly and religious vocations. I pray that each of them is blessed, as I have been, with support of family and friends which will give them the grace and courage to answer his call with certitude. GOD STILL CALLS!

✤ FIFTEEN ✤

Shannon Lucht
As I Recall Him

Over the years I had received and approved applications from men with degrees in mechanical engineering, law enforcement, education, agriculture, music, and sociology. Some are now in the seminary and others are ordained. I had never, however, had an application from a student in pharmacy. That is, not until May of 1994. It was in late April of that year that one of our good pastors wrote to tell me that a young man in his parish had shown signs of being interested in the seminary. He supplied the name and address of the person and I immediately wrote to him and invited him to come to my office for a visit.

The young man's name was Shannon Lucht and he was completing his fifth year of college studies to be a pharmacist. Shannon came to see me within the next month and poured out his soul to me. He told me that he had thought of priesthood when he was younger. He had been a devout altar boy for many years and his parents and family were devout Catholics. Together they had given Shannon an excellent foundation of religious education and practice and his faith was strong. He had two brothers and two sisters and the family was very close.

Although his interest in priesthood had waned during his later high school years and during the first years of college, lately it had become steadily stronger once again. Shannon needed to talk to someone and he told me that he had found a priest near the University with whom he could visit and ask questions about his vocation. It was all providential, as God's ways always are.

We visited at great length, on that occasion, about his life and where God may be leading him. The tug at his heart was real and he needed to respond. He was really ready to enter the seminary the next year but since his pharmacy degree was so close, Shannon thought that he should finish his degree work and then begin his theology. His parents concurred with this decision and so did I. In the meantime, Shannon had heard of the Vianney Program at Cardinal Muench Seminary where he could live without commitment and continue his pharmacy classes.

In the meantime, Shannon was attending daily Mass and receiving Holy Communion and his prayer life was growing stronger every day. He was also working as a chef at a local restaurant and trying hard to keep up with his classes. It was not an easy life for him but he was determined that he would finish his degree work and then enter the seminary. During the months that followed, Shannon and I kept a close and steady line of communication going. His enthusiasm was catching and he came to know and enjoy other seminarians in our area.

Once his classes were completed, it was necessary for Shannon to spend a year as an intern in various pharmacies for the necessary experience in order to graduate. This meant more delays and more patient waiting to enter the seminary. During this year we made arrangements with pastors for Shannon to live in some of the rectories of our diocese and so become acquainted with some of our priests and their lifestyles. It was a real "internship" for him in more ways than one and he thrived on the experience. This arrangement made it convenient for Shannon to continue his spiritual life while completing his requirements for graduation. At the same time, his vocation was deepening and his desire to enter the seminary and become a priest

126

became stronger. He saw, first hand, the life we live as priests, the people we serve, and the joy of ministry. He also saw the hard work which our priests do and the long hours they keep. It was a time of testing his vocation and, with the grace of God again, his response continued to be strong.

Finally, the day arrived in May of 1996 when Shannon graduated with a doctor of pharmacy degree. That summer Shannon completed and passed his board exams and became a licensed pharmacist. While he was tempted with the thought that he was now in a position to get a good job and make good money to pay off his education bills, his longing to enter the seminary and become a priest was stronger and the "moment of grace" had come.

At last, in the fall of 1996, Shannon entered pre-theology and began a five year program to prepare for ordination. He had been able to take some necessary classes in philosophy during his time in the Vianney Program so now he could complete his studies and be a priest in five instead of six years.

Shannon's determination has been an inspiration to everyone. His close friendship with our priests and seminarians has impressed all who know him. He has been regular and consistent in attending seminarian gatherings and activities in the diocese and sometimes he is called upon to exercise his culinary gifts and talents. Even the seminary recognized those gifts when he was appointed director of banquets for the second year of his theology.

Sometimes our students are called upon to make a real sacrifice for the sake of their calling. This is the case with Shannon. He could be a successful pharmacist. He could be enjoying a high salaried job and have money to pay his bills. Instead he is doing what God wants him to do and there will be other ways to meet his bills and expenses. Shannon's great faith and deep conviction will carry him through. He is now in his third year of theology and will be ordained after just two more years of classes. It has been a long journey and many hours of class work and prayer time.

Perseverence is a common word for Shannon. It has gained respect and admiration for him and rightly so. His good judgment, sense of humor and common sense will serve him well in his future ministry. And in God's own mysterious way, ALL of Shannon's years of education will be of use in a multitude of ways. God has plans for him!

Shannon's Story...In His Own Words....

I would say that I come from your average Catholic family. I was an altar boy at my home parish of St. Thomas in Tioga, North Dakota, and served Mass regularly. The first serious thoughts I had about being a priest came when I was a junior in high school. I first noticed these thoughts at Mass during the prayers of intercession after the homily. One of the prayers the priest would say was for an increase of vocations to the priesthood and religious life.

When Father said that prayer, there was this little voice in my head saying, "You should do this," or "this is for you." The next week the same thing would happen. This scared me. I remember just trying to ignore it and put the thought out of my mind.

Whenever that thought about the priesthood would come, I would try everything I could to get it out of my head. I remember getting upset at God for this constant pestering. I'd tell him, "Find someone else," or "I don't want to do it," or "why are you asking me anyway, being a priest isn't the cool thing to do and besides, priests don't make any money!" I think this last reason was the big one. Growing up in a family where we didn't have much for extras, I was determined to have a career that made good money and the priesthood wasn't one of those careers.

Well, this little battle continued and I kept it all to myself. One day during the fall of my senior year of high school, I was talking about college with my mom. I was telling her that I didn't know what I should go into and she asked me if I had prayed about it. "Have you asked God what he wants you to do?" I don't remember what I told her but I surely didn't want to ask God what to do because I knew he would tell me to become a priest, and I wasn't going to do that!

Later, in my senior year, I happened to be in the guidance counselor's office and I saw a pamphlet about a career in pharmacy. I read the pamphlet and started thinking. I knew the pharmacist in my hometown and his career seemed appealing to me. Well, that was it. I was going to be a pharmacist. I went to Bismarck State College for my two years of pre-pharmacy and then was accepted into pharmacy school at North Dakota State University in Fargo.

Things seemed to be going along very nicely. The thought of priesthood had left my mind. In fact, after a couple of years in Fargo, I had pretty much stopped practicing my faith all together. I didn't just wake up one day and decide that I wasn't going to pray or go to Mass anymore, it was a gradual process. One Sunday I didn't go to Mass for whatever reason. Several weeks later I missed Sunday Mass again. It became easier and easier to not go to Mass and pretty soon I wasn't praying or going to Mass at all.

On Ash Wednesday of 1994, I was watching television in my apartment when my roommate asked me if I was going to Mass with him. For some reason I must have felt guilty so I went. We ended up going to a parish in Fargo that I didn't even know was there. After going to Mass that evening, I didn't pray or attend Mass at all during the rest of Lent.

On Tuesday of Holy Week, I was walking home from class when a thought entered my mind: "What the heck are you doing? You aren't praying, you aren't going to Mass, you're hanging around with friends who are a bad influence on you. This was not the way you were brought up!" By the time I reached my apartment I knew that I had to come back to the Lord. The first thing I knew I had to do was go to confession. I found out that I had missed all of the communal reconciliation services in town and I couldn't make an appointment until after Easter. Needless to say, I was pretty disappointed.

When I got home from class on Holy Thursday, something told me to try calling the parish that I attended on Ash Wednesday, and so I did. The priest didn't have time before Mass that evening but he told me to come to Mass and he would hear my confession afterward. That is what I did. I was very nervous about going to confession because I hadn't been there for so long, But I managed to put those fears aside. After my confession as I was praying in the church, I felt this unusual peace come over me. I felt a strong desire to pray and I knew that I was in the presence of God.

Then the thoughts of the priesthood came flooding back into my mind again, only much stronger than they ever were before. I thought back to high school and all the times I tried to ignore his calling and I just prayed, "God, if you want me to become a priest, I will do it."

At the time I finally said "yes" to God, I still had two years of pharmacy school left. After talking to my parents and vocation director, I decided that I should finish pharmacy school. I graduated in May of 1996 with a doctor of pharmacy degree. That fall I entered St. Meinrad Seminary in southern Indiana.

I have completed three years of study there and have two more to go. God-willing I will be ordained a priest in the summer of 2001. It is true....GOD STILL CALLS!!!!

SIXTEEN

Michael Kautzman
As I Recall Him

Some priests are very good at watching for signs of priestly or religious vocations among the young people of their parishes. Vocation directors receive many notes and letters, and even references in casual conversations with priests about certain "ones" as possible "candidates." A few anxious and overzealous priests see vocations everywhere. Others seldom mention the subject at all.

All of these "tips" need to be weighed and tested. Not every clue is a real one, nor are they all to be ignored. One such reference kept coming to my office about a young man attending one of our state universities who was showing up more and more for daily Mass at one of the local parishes. The pastor was known for his good pastoral qualities and his interest in young people who expressed a love of the Lord in their daily and weekly practice of their Catholic Faith. It was from him that the message kept coming to me that this young man showed "the right signs."

Michael Kautzman is the oldest in a family of six children and his parents are both devout Catholics. I had known Mike's younger brother, Steve, since it was he who first came to my office to visit about the seminary. Both Steve and Mike were involved in youth work in their home parish and community and Steve was very active in Teens for Life. Steve decided to try the seminary by entering the

131

Vianney Program at Cardinal Muench Seminary in Fargo, North Dakota. He stayed there one year and then decided that this was not his vocation–at least not just now.

Working with Steve had acquainted me somewhat with the Kautzman family and so when I heard that Mike was beginning to attend daily Mass and was also involved in parish activities for young people, I phoned him at the university and we visited. It is always a gamble when a vocation director asks a young man by phone if he would be willing to come to the vocation office to visit about his future. Very often the answer is "no," or at least there is some obvious hesitation which also speaks loudly and clearly. It is so easy to say "no" on the phone. In this case, however, as in those pleasant few, Mike was anxious to come. On Saturday, February 26, 1994, we met for the first time.

I remember being very impressed by this young man. Mike was attending college at the time and working towards a degree in education. His goal was to teach and do some coaching. Mike was very athletic. He had participated in a variety of sports in high school and had also played football during his college days. He enjoyed working with young people and thought that he would like to use his education degree for a year or two in teaching and coaching before entering the seminary. He was presently involved in student teaching and would graduate that spring.

Looking to the future, Mike and I could see how God might be working in his life. His teaching experience and his interest in young people could serve him very well as a young priest. He was excited about that prospect and we visited at length about his prayer life and his attraction to the priestly life.

He could feel the "tug at his heart" and it was growing stronger all the time. Mike had been dating but it was nothing serious and he felt more and more that his call was to celibacy and priesthood.

In my "memo" of that day in February, I wrote, "We discussed priesthood and celibacy at quite some length and I was very

132

impressed with Michael's understanding of the commitment of celibacy and also his willingness to live it. His understanding of celibacy as a grace and not a burden is very important. I was also impressed by his desire to be a good priest and to serve the spiritual needs of others. He has a very strong prayer life and has promised to continue his prayer life according to the free time that he has during these next weeks of student teaching."

Michael graduated from college that spring and took a job teaching in a small community not far from Fargo. He did well that year and enjoyed being with the young people. As the year moved on, however, the desire to enter the seminary became stronger and stronger. God was working in his life and Mike needed to make a tough decision.

Should he give up his good paying job and promising future as a teacher and coach and enter the seminary or should he continue for a few more years and make some money? He knew that when he entered the seminary, as is the case for all seminarians, the income stops. He also had college bills to pay. What should he do? We visited at length over the course of that year and on May 31 of 1995, Mike was ready to decide. He would complete his teaching position at the end of this school year and not renew his contract. His vocation was too strong. He would not be at peace until he tried the seminary.

That September, Mike was ready to go back to college and begin his journey to the priesthood. The "moment of grace" had come and Mike had responded wholeheartedly. He would enter pre-theology and spend two more years in a college seminary before his would have the required credits in language and philosophy to begin his theology. No matter, Mike was very certain of his calling and ready to begin the process of education and spiritual formation required.

The disciplined years of athletic involvement, years of classroom work and years of personal prayer convinced Mike that he could do it. And he did it very well. After two years in pre-theology, Mike is now in his third year of theology and will be ordained a priest, God willing, in just one more year after this one.

Like most seminarians, Mike's strong devotion to Our Blessed Mother has been an added source of comfort and strength for him through the years. His manly and genuine love of Christ and his church is deep and strong. He knows who he is and is comfortable with human weakness as part of the human condition, but at the same time he trusts in his own goodness and that of others. Mike is "solid" in the good sense of the term.

Mike is greatly respected by his classmates and peers. He is always ready to be part of any program or activity suggested by the seminary or the vocation office. Being the oldest member of his family, Mike shows great maturity and good sense in his approach to life. He also shows that same spiritual maturity and good judgment in his approach to God's call. He looks forward to serving God's people, especially the young with whom he has a special rapport, as teacher, counselor, and friend. Some day Mike will be a very good pastor--caring and compassionate. We all look forward to his priestly ministry and, with God's grace, he will not disappoint us.

Mike's Story.....In His Own Words...

It seems like in so many other vocation stories, one begins to see an interesting story develop only upon reflection. Oftentimes, as the story is unfolding, one is not fully aware of the significance of the events which are occurring in the everyday pattern of one's life.

I think the seeds of my vocation were planted by my family. It was always made known to me that I should be open to whatever God called me to be, and my parents encouraged me to make all the options available when searching out my vocation.

Through the good example of my parents' faith, their support of religious vocations and their decision to send me to a Catholic school,

I was graced with the opportunity to see the work of faithful priests and nuns up close. I always respected their commitment and life of prayer and service to others, so at an early age I can remember considering the religious life as a serious option. I can remember times of "playing Mass" with my younger brother and sister at home.

As I grew older and entered high school, the idea of the religious life faded a bit. However, I do remember a number of people, including some of my peers, mentioning that I should think about becoming a priest. I always took this as a compliment, but did not take it as seriously as I would later in life. I continued to have great respect for the priests I knew.

Looking back, I think the sacrament of reconciliation played a role in my vocation. I remember being thankful, knowing that no matter what I was struggling with in my life, there was a place I could go and talk about it with someone who would not only give me good advice, but help me to overcome these struggles by offering me a sacramental sign of the mercy and forgiveness of a loving God. It seems that each of the priests I turned to through the various stages of my life helped me greatly and I respected them very much for that. I enjoyed my high school career playing athletics, dating and spending a lot of time with my friends.

When it came time for college, I was unsure of what God was calling me to do. I was given an opportunity to play football at Dickinson State University, and since athletics was something I enjoyed very much, I decided to attend college there, play football and study to be a teacher and coach. My time at DSU was great. I met a lot of good friends and had a great time. Although I was having a good time, I still felt there was something missing. Toward the end of my time there, I began to get an inner feeling that God was called me to something. It is a feeling I can't fully explain but it was a mixture of joy and hope for the future (even though I had no idea of what the future would bring). I began to pray to God that he would help me find the vocation to which he was calling me. I began to go to daily Mass on a regular basis at St. Patrick's Parish in Dickinson and pray the mysteries of the rosary.

It was about this time that my brother decided to enter the seminary and he invited me to a "live-in weekend." I can remember being a bit hesitant because it was in the spring and there were many fun things going on during the weekends at college. I didn't want to "miss anything." Also, I was unsure of what the seminary was like. I wondered whether it would be a boring weekend.

I was surprised to find that it was anything but boring. The guys there were great and many of them had been very successful in other areas of work before entering the seminary. I remember being impressed with the fact that they had given up their former careers to try the seminary. I was also impressed by their personalities. They were people I would look up to no matter what vocation they were pursuing. It was after this weekend that I began to think seriously, "Hey, I could do this!"

I returned to school with a sense of excitement. Maybe this is what I am being called to. However, I only had one year left at DSU to complete my degree and since I had always wanted to teach and coach, I decided to spend at least one year doing that before making any final decisions about the seminary.

I got a job teaching and coaching track and basketball at Oriska Public School in a small North Dakota town. I enjoyed teaching and coaching very much that year, but as the year continued, I began to have a stronger and stronger feeling that I was being called to explore the seminary. By the end of my first year of teaching, I contacted, Msgr. Walsh, the vocation director, to begin the application process. I can still remember the day in May when I took my teaching contract down to the post office and pushed it into the box --unsigned. I was scheduled for a good raise and had enjoyed my life living independently. Watching the letter fall into the box was a little scary. However, it turned out to be the right decision.

I went to Cardinal Muench Seminary in the fall and really fell in love with the place. It was a great experience. Actually, it was a "no lose" situation. I was able to explore my vocation more fully through the help of spiritual direction and formation, was opened up to a whole new way of looking at the world through philosophy, learned much more about my Catholic faith, continued to be involved in athletics, and met many new wonderful people.

Even if I had found that God was calling me to something else, my time there would not have been wasted. I continue to feel God calling me to pursue the priesthood and I am now in the third year of theology at St. Paul Seminary in St. Paul, Minnesota. I enjoy the continual new challenges that arise and more and more I look forward to coming back home to our diocese to serve the people there. Hopefully, I will be able to become involved with some teaching and coaching again in the future.

The journey God has led me on has been a very exciting one. I would encourage any young person who has any sense of curiosity about the religious life to explore it as an option. Even if you find that God is calling you to something else, you will gain from your experience considering a religious vocation.

SEVENTEEN

Chad Gion As I Recall Him

In one of my other seminarian's stories, I quoted part of the Diocesan Vocation Prayer which has been in use in our diocese for fifty years or more. Our people are devout in their faith and deeply believe in what they pray for. Another part of that prayer goes like this, "Give to parents that faith, love and spirit of sacrifice which will inspire them to offer their sons and daughters to God's service and cause them to rejoice exceedingly whenever one of their family is called to the religious life..." This part of the prayer is not often well received by some parents. They find it difficult to accept the fact that their son or daughter might be called to be a priest, brother or sister in religious life. And not many parents actually OFFER their children to God's service in that real sense of sacrifice.

I don't know how seriously Chad Gion's parents, Don and Bonnie Gion, interpreted that prayer. I also don't know for sure if they consciously offered their children to God's service in the church. I do know that they did their best to provide the kind of home and family life from which vocations might spring. They have always been serious about their Catholic faith, consistently involved in parish and church activities, and working religiously at their marriage to make it a happy and holy example of commitment and sacred vow.

Chad is the oldest of five children. I have known him since he was about five years old. His parents and I served together as team members for Marriage Encounter Weekends some years ago. We have been close friends ever since. For this reason, although I recognized many signs of a vocation in Chad's life as he grew up, I hesitated to exert much influence on his future plans. I did not want to over influence him. Both his parents and I prayed that he would come to his own decision in his own good time.

Chad is musically gifted, along with many other special talents, and was involved in a musical youth group throughout high school and his early college years. This was his outlet–his way of expressing his faith and his devotion. Much of the group's music was sacred.

Chad was also involved in SEARCH and, along with his parents, took part in a number of weekends in different capacities. In fact, it was our diocesan youth director, who is also the Search director, who first told me that Chad was beginning to seriously consider the priesthood as his vocation. The time had come for the vocation director to make his move.

I called Chad at his dorm and we decided to meet for a visit. It was March 25, 1995, the Feast of the Annunciation, the Feast of Our Blessed Mother's surrender to God's message as she agreed to "let it be done to me according to thy will".....she would become the Mother of Jesus.

The challenge of music was very close to Chad's heart and he was involved in a good music program in college. The tug at his heart, however, was becoming stronger and stronger. Chad was puzzled and confused. He was torn between two loves. We visited from time to time and yet never came to any serious consideration of the seminary that summer.

In the fall, Chad returned to college and continued to pursue the study of music. It was a turbulent semester. Doubts and fears kept plaguing him. Dorm life was becoming unbearable. Chad once told me that "all they do at the dorm is drink and party." Yes, it was college life with a vengeance, but through it all came a consistent voice and it was growing louder and louder. It was the voice of Christ–a voice often drowned in the noise of life, but sometimes recognized and listened to in prayer and quiet times. That is what made the difference: Chad's prayer life and moments of deep reflection. No one was pushing. Only the nudge of grace - begging for a response.

It was during that Christmas vacation that Chad came to see me. He was looking for peace. He was searching for meaning in his life. He was unsettled and unhappy. His music no longer filled the void in his heart. He was attracted to seminary life, yet he did not want it to be just an escape from a painful situation. He wanted to do the right thing. He wanted to do what God wanted him to do. Should he enter the seminary? Could he enter at the semester and not wait until the next academic year? To wait might mean the loss of his vocation. The "moment of grace" had come. Now was the time to begin the journey.

After some serious phone calls to the seminary rector and some re-arranging of Chad's plans, he was ready to attend the mid-term retreat and begin his seminary life in just one week. As a starter, Chad decided to enter the Vianney Program for that first semester and if everything worked out, he would formally apply for acceptance as a seminarian for the next year. It did not take long before Chad knew that he was in the right place. He found peace. He was at home.

Soon the other students recognized the giftedness of this young man. His outgoing personality and his good sense of humor made him a popular companion at the seminary. He did well academically and was serious about the discipline of prayer and study. He felt his vocation grow stronger and, as the months went by, he became anxious to begin his theology. Chad's kindness and care are well known among his peers.

His preparation for a happy and holy priesthood is taken seriously, even though, in lighter moments, Chad can be the life of the party. He is bright and intelligent and very effective in working with young people.

Parents, like Don and Bonnie Gion, who do not push but rather offer their children to God's service, and encourage them quietly and sincerely with prayer and moral support, are tremendously important in the whole vocation program. Chad is a very fortunate young man, like most of our seminarians, in that he comes from such a strong Catholic family background.

He is now in his second year of theology and has two more years after this one until, God willing, ordination to the priesthood. Time will go fast and day by day Chad will continue to respond to God's grace like Our Blessed Mother on the Feast of the Annunciation. His own mother and Our Blessed Mother will quietly pray him into becoming more and more like Christ, the Son of God, whose priest he will soon be. Chad's heart is ready--and mothers are like that. "He who is mighty has done great things for me, and holy is his name." (*Magnificat*).

Chad's Story...In His Own Words....

I have spent little time thinking about my vocation. Through the twists and turns of life, through my doubts and fears, I have always known that I would spend time studying in a seminary. Knowing that, I did not worry what the future might hold because I knew (at least in part) what it would bring.

The first time I considered the priesthood was as a child. I might have been seven or eight years old. Following Sunday Mass, our family took a trip to Mott, a town near my home. I do not remember why we were traveling there, but I do remember that while en route, Mom mentioned that a woman in the parish had recommended my name to those who were promoting Called By Name. This is a program which seeks to identify anyone who may have a vocation to the priesthood or religious life.

I knew nothing of Called By Name. I knew nothing about the priesthood. I did not even know the woman very well who recommended me. This did not keep me from feeling excited about the news. Someone I hardly knew believed that she recognized in me something which she thought was "priestly," whatever that meant.

I had never given the priesthood any thought. I tried to remember what I had seen Father Pete Kramer, our parish priest, do to keep busy. The only work I could remember him doing was saying Mass on Sundays and weekdays and hearing the confessions of all the CCD students before Easter and Christmas. I could not imagine what else he did, but I thought that it would probably take a lot of time to work up the nerve to stand in front of all those people every morning at Mass, leading and preaching, so I figured he probably spent a lot of time being nervous. I had no difficulty imagining how busy that might keep me.

I also recognized the amount of respect Father Kramer received from the parishioners. I did not know what he did to deserve that respect, but the thought of receiving such respect myself was both awesome and terrifying. "Who am I," I thought, "to be shown such respect?" I saw how people I respected, respected this man about whom I knew little. I did not understand why he deserved such respect.

In spite of my vast ignorance, from that time on I knew that I would end up as a priest somehow. I never inquired with anyone about how one goes about becoming a priest. I told no one about my decision. I felt no need to talk to anyone. I was a bit embarrassed by my realization. Really, how many children feel an innate knowledge that they are called to the priesthood? It struck me as bizarre, so I kept my thoughts to myself. I was also afraid of this call to a vocation, a vocation which I did not understand at all. I thought that if I kept it to myself, maybe my conviction would fade. To express to someone else my thoughts would make this craziness more difficult to put behind me, should my mind change. My mind was simultaneously moving in two directions. I thought about this call that I knew I had and how it might be answered, and I thought about when it would go away, afraid of what it meant for me.

In later adolescence I modified the way I understood the call. Instead of called to the priesthood, I told myself that I was called to try the seminary and discern the priesthood. Such a change in my understanding of the call was in part an indicator of a more mature understanding of how a vocation is discerned. It was also a defense from the call itself. A call to seminary to discern the priesthood is more palatable than a call to the priesthood itself.

I still had not talked with anyone about what I had known for years. In retrospect, I am amazed that I told no one for almost twelve years about my call, especially in light of how much I have discussed it since entering the seminary. I still felt simultaneously that God's call was undeniable but absolutely crazy.

For a young man just finishing high school and about to enter college, religion and all that the life of the priest includes were not particularly fun to think about. I was becoming more involved in music, especially punk and related genres. I was teaching myself how to play the guitar and drums, and played in a band with two friends from Mott. Playing music quickly became the most important thing in my life.

When I graduated from high school I attended the school where my "band mates" were--Moorhead, Minnesota--so that the rockin' might continue. We played shows around the Fargo-Moorhead area, and when we were on stage playing, I loved what I was doing. When we were not playing or practicing, I was not as happy with my life. Many of the friends I made were drifting and I did not expect they would reach land soon. The world they and I inhabited was one of no truth, only individual perceptions of truth.

One might have a belief system, but it would be inappropriate to suggest that there was objective truth. This was especially true with regards to moral and theological issues. I soon began to seriously explore my understanding of the world and God's place in it. The friends with whom I surrounded myself generally understood the universe as purely materialistic. God may or may not exist. And even if he did, he wasn't involved in what was going on in the world. The universe was simply chemicals mixing and rocks bouncing off one another. There was nothing spiritual about it.

Going into college, I began questioning what had been for me basic suppositions about the world around me. God's existence and his relationship to the world were not clear to me.

A definitive moment in my formation as a Christian came one night in my dorm room. It was probably two or three in the morning and I had been spending a lot of time thinking about what I believed. As I lay in bed, I thought about what in this world was really worth living for. If the universe is just a huge chemical mixing bowl and we humans are no more than our chemical components, I questioned why I should put up with any suffering or pain....why I should not just end my life? If we are simply chemicals, then no experience or action is more than a biochemical reaction of some sort. All of our emotions, all of our thoughts are no more than chemistry.

I thought of the love I knew my parents had for me. If I killed myself, what would it do to them? They would be devastated, certainly, and hurting them that much would generally deter me from taking such a drastic action. But if their emotions and their love for me were nothing but the fortuitous mixture of chemicals, then why should I feel particularly concerned about their feelings? Their pain would be nothing but a chemical reaction. I do not care about chemical reaction.

I decided that the most important emotion, the deepest experience I had had in life was love from family and friends and my love for my family and friends. My love for them and their love for me was the primary reason I would be willing to live a life which would certainly include deep pain and sorrow. But only if we are more than chemicals; if our love for one another is somehow more than mere chemistry; then there is something to live for. Relationships had to be more than individuals reacting to one another chemically. If we also interacted on a spiritual level, I found myself willing to live in a world in which there is pain and suffering, even if it is my pain and suffering.

Given a spiritual side to this world, it is possible to imagine that there is some purpose to what is going on around us, even if that purpose is not always clear. I also felt the deep truth that God is love. God as love was part of every relationship in my life. Love for my friends and family and their love for me was the primary reason that I found life worth living, and God was this love. I discovered God all around me in relationships with loved ones. This was a very important realization. God is not some being outside the human sphere. God is always present in us and in our relationships with others, making my life possible and worth living.

After that night, I realized that in spite of how much I loved playing in a band, my life needed to change. I discovered that the situations I placed myself in had an effect on me, even if I did not fully participate in what was going on around me. I had surrounded myself with friends who had no hope, and that hopelessness took root in me. I fought through it that night in my dorm room, but I knew that I needed to move on to something new. I knew that the time to enter the seminary was approaching. In the fall of 1995, I transferred to the other school in Fargo, NDSU. I knew that to attend Cardinal Muench Seminary, a minor seminary in Fargo, I had to attend NDSU because the two were affiliated. I was still afraid, however, to take that next step--entering the seminary. I knew that I had to, but still resisted. I lived on the campus of NDSU that fall. By the end of that semester I decided that I was going to either drop out of school for a while until I figured out what to do, or I would enter the seminary, which I knew I should do.

During the Christmas break of that year, I met with Msgr. Walsh and asked him about entering the seminary. He had mentioned many times the possibility of my entering the seminary, so when I called, he acted quickly. Within days I was accepted as a seminarian for the diocese and a student at Cardinal Muench Seminary.

Having now spent some time in the seminary, I understand just how out of the ordinary my entrance into the seminary was. I did not take any psychological tests before I entered. These came later. I did not have any pre-entrance interviews with the seminary. I just showed up at the seminary retreat at the end of the Christmas break and was accepted on the weight of Msgr. Walsh's recommendations.

This is essentially how I ended up in the seminary. For me, it had been about recognizing and accepting the call from God to serve him. I have been more or less willing to follow his lead at different times, as I am more or less thankful for where God is calling me at different times. I am still dealing with the question, "What have I done to deserve this?" I continue to work on understanding God's call to priesthood as an honor, which it certainly is. I have also asked this question feeling the call to be a burden.

Growing in preparation for ordination has often been as painful as it has been rewarding. I have changed a great deal since the first time I thought about the priesthood, but that initial confidence which I felt about my call has remained intact.

I have now completed three years of seminary formation and have three years remaining. God willing, at the completion of these years of education, I will be ordained a priest. The woman who recommended me to the Called By Name Program so many years ago was right!

EIGHTEEN

James Link As I Recall Him

In the magnificent poetic classic by Francis Thompson entitled, *The Hound of Heaven*, we read of the relentless pursuit of the Hound of Heaven after those whom he seeks. Putting this image into a vocation perspective, it is the Lord Jesus who pursues, "with unhurrying chase, and unperturbed pace, deliberate speed, and majestic instancy." The poet skillfully describes the flight of the soul from "those strong feet which followed, after," until at last the surrender takes place and "that voice is around me like a bursting sea.... Ah, fondest, blindest, weakest, I am he whom thou seekest."

We can all find something of ourselves and our own restlessness in this beautiful poem. And for some it will mean even more than for others. James Link, a talented and pleasant young man has known the pursuit of the Hound of Heaven. He has wrestled spiritually and mentally, and, yes, even physically, with the desire and yet persistent doubts remained which sometimes plague him.

It was Thursday, May 26, 1994, when James Link came to my office to visit about his vocation. It was more of an exploratory visit than a time for decision and commitment. We visited at length about a possible vocation to the priesthood for James. His pastors had always been members of the Benedictine Abbey and so he had spent a week there, thinking that perhaps that would be where God wanted him to serve. He came away rather certain that religious life was not the kind of priesthood he might be called to live. He was not familiar with diocesan priesthood but was willing to learn.

Was God calling him to be a priest? James had many gifts and talents and certainly gave signs of a possible vocation. He was a gentle and caring soul and had a ready smile which attracted people to him in a genuine positive way. He was and is a very personable young man, friendly and out-going....good qualities for a future priest. I encouraged him to continue to pray about his future and open his heart to the voice of Christ. Listening carefully for direction is essential. James promised to do this and to keep in touch.

Soon after that visit, James came to my office again and informed me that he was ready to enter the seminary and would like to begin in September. The "moment of grace" had come and James had responded. He completed all of the necessary paper work and seemed certain of his choice. He had been accepted as a seminarian for our diocese and the seminary was waiting for him.

On July 15th I received a phone call from the rector of the seminary where James had been registered. He told me that James had called him to say that he had changed his mind and would not be entering the seminary there in September. Surprise! I called James right away to see what had changed his mind and he informed me that he had been speaking with some other priests and now felt that his vocation was to the Benedictine Abbey. If that was where the Lord was leading James, I did not want to stand in the way. At the same time, James seemed confused and doubtful about his whole situation. I asked him to consider following his plan to enter the seminary in September to see if this might be his vocation. Since everything was in order for his entrance to the seminary I took this as a sign that God wanted him there. At the same time I suggested to James that he could continue his discernment process about religious life versus diocesan priesthood in the seminary. He did not promise to do this but consented to pray about it and be open to God's grace.

James did not enter the seminary, nor did he apply to the Abbey that first semester. He continued in college though and just before Christmas he called for an appointment to discuss the possibility of entering the seminary at the semester break in the middle of the year. This was not the usual practice but the seminary staff welcomed James in January, and he settled in to prepare himself for the priesthood. His seminary journey had begun and he seemed relieved, content and at peace.

The semester went by quickly and just as it was coming to a close James wrote me a long letter explaining why he was leaving the seminary at the end of the semester. I asked him to come for a visit, which he graciously did, and we visited about his letter. James had made up his mind. Nothing would change it. I encouraged him to keep in touch with me and our seminarians and continue to be open to the Lord's voice. James was unsettled again but felt that he was doing the right thing.

We kept in touch over the next couple of years. In the meantime, James was quite convinced that his vocation was not to the priesthood. In fact, he began dating and was soon seriously considering the vocation of marriage. His fiancee was a wonderful Catholic girl. They were soon engaged and had set the wedding date. As the time drew near, however, James became less and less certain of what he was doing. Attending daily Mass together and praying together kept the persistent image of priesthood in his thoughts. He was seriously attracted.

"With unhurrying chase, and unperturbed pace, deliberate speed and majestic instancy...." James was haunted by thoughts of priesthood. With proper counseling and good spiritual direction, James finally came to the conclusion that marriage, at least at this time, was not for him. His fiancee was understanding and supportive in his decision. Many others were not. They thought that he has made his decision to marry and that he should stay with it. It was a most difficult time for

James. He felt abandoned by almost everyone. He sought consolation in the church, where he decided he must serve as a priest at last.

Another struggle. Another decision. Another change of plans and re-arrangement of his life and activities. James graduated with a degree in social work and within weeks entered the seminary in pre-theology as a student for the diocese. The "Hound of Heaven" had overtaken James and he had, again, surrendered. It has been a painful and difficult journey for this talented and gifted young man with the ready smile.

James has much to give to the priestly ministry and God will make the most of his many attributes. Not everyone struggles so hard nor so perseveringly to know God's will and to follow it Some give up more easily and never find their destiny. Not every vocation is so difficult to discern. It has been a long and hard journey and it is not over yet. James will have three more years of theology after this one. May those years be years of grace and peace. May they bring comfort and contentment and the definite conviction that this is, indeed, where God wants James to be because he has work for him to do in the Kingdom of God which no one else can do

James' Story...In His Own Words....

The poem, *The Hound of Heaven*, does indeed echo profoundly in my heart and soul as I reflect upon my own vocation discernment and how I have continually felt the presence of God's call in my life. I, too, have experienced the Divine Chase in which the Lord remains steadfast and unrelenting in his pursuit. Yet, I remained equally steadfast in resisting him.

On Thursday, May 26, 1994, when I first paid a visit to the vocation office, I had not given the idea of a priestly vocation much thought. Although I was raised in a devoutly Catholic family in southwestern North Dakota, I never gave any serious consideration to the priesthood. In fact, during my high school years, the idea of a priestly vocation was the farthest thing from my mind. I was more interested in friends, sports and girls.

It was during my freshman year in college, however, that I had a grace-filled moment in which I began to understand that my relationship with Christ entailed more than what I had previously been giving. I began to attend daily Mass, frequented the sacrament of penance, and the inner desire to continually give more to the Lord persisted.

After I finished the spring semester at the University of North Dakota in Grand Forks, I decided to meet with Msgr. Walsh and discuss what I had been feeling and experiencing over the past months. We visited at length about a possible vocation to the priesthood.

My pastors had always been members of the Benedictine Abbey at Richardton, North Dakota, so I spent a week there, thinking that perhaps that would be where God wanted me to serve. I came away feeling that religious life was not where the Lord was leading me at this point in my life.

Over the summer I gave much thought and prayer to the possibility of attending the seminary in the fall or spending more time at the Abbey. It was a difficult decision for me and as fall approached, so I decided to do neither and simply continued on with school. Yet, the persistent feeling of giving myself to God in the priesthood continued to dwell within my heart, so I gathered up the strength and decided to finally enter the seminary after Christmas.

The semester went by quickly and everything seemed to be going fine, except for my intense desire to someday have a wife and family. For me, this desire was, is, and probably always will be my biggest struggle. Growing up in a close-knit and loving family gave me a view of married life that was both attractive and hard to let go of. I fought the idea of priesthood even though it had gained a place deep within my heart. I resisted and as the semester was coming to a close, I decided that the seminary was not the place for me at this time. I wanted to get my degree in social work and see where that road would lead. I wrote a long letter to Msgr. Walsh, explaining why I was leaving and we later visited about my decision. He encouraged me to keep in touch with both him and our seminarians and to continue to be open to the Lord's voice. I agreed to do both.

After leaving the seminary, I started dating a wonderful young woman whom I had known from my childhood, and all the signs seemed to be indicating that my vocation was to be in the sacrament of marriage. Tonya and I dated for three years and became engaged. She was a woman of great faith and love for God and, as much as I knew it would break both of our hearts to postpone the engagement, I still had the inner feeling that the Lord was calling me to the priesthood or the religious life.

This was a very difficult time in my life as I had a strong, healthy relationship with a wonderful Catholic woman whom I wanted to marry. Yet I knew there was something else tugging at my heart. Attending daily Mass together and praying together kept the persistent image of the priesthood in my thoughts. I was once again caught, "with unhurrying chase, unperturbed pace, deliberate speed and majestic instancy..." Tonya and I both prayed a great deal, sought spiritual direction from our parish priest, and after months of discernment, we both decided that I needed to return to the seminary.

This was the most spiritually, emotionally, and physically exhausting period in my life. Not only was this decision going to affect me, but also my fiancee, my family and friends, and all who had come to know us as a happy and loving couple. I could not make sense of my feelings and emotions. Was I just experiencing cold feet? Was I running from commitment? Was the Lord really asking me to forsake marriage in order to follow him unreservedly in the priesthood? Life seemed to be in turmoil. Family and friends found it difficult to understand my indecision and questioned whether or not I was making the right decision about returning to the seminary. I felt alone and misunderstood.

It was, however, during those months of anguish when I became increasingly drawn to prayer in the presence of the Blessed Sacrament. When I was before the Lord in the Holy Eucharist, it seemed as though my troubles faded away and for a brief moment I was at peace. I remember how the little Blessed Sacrament Chapel in Our Lady of Grace Church became a place of solitude and peace amidst the storm of self-doubt, sorrow and uncertainty.

A religious vocation is truly a mystery and I will always believe that my own mystery became more clear during those visits to Our Lord in the Blessed Sacrament Another surrender. Another change of plans and rearrangement of my life and activities.

I graduated with a degree in social work and within weeks entered Kenrick-Glennon Seminary in St. Louis, enrolled in the pre-theology program. That was a year and a half ago and this fall I will be started second theology.

The past year and a half have not been without their struggles and doubts. It took me a long time to get over the loss of my relationship with Tonya and the plans we had made for the future. I am still dealing with that to this day. Yet, I have deeply enjoyed my time and studies at Kenrick and I feel that this is, indeed, where the Lord is calling me.

Despite the struggles, I feel a sense of inner peace that I could have never experienced without taking this step. My faith journey has shown me that the more one surrenders his life to God, the more he will fill it with his own Divine Love. I increasingly look forward to my priestly ordination in three more years and the day when I can fully proclaim that God is faithful and steadfast in his promises.

NINETEEN

James Shea As I Recall Him

In the Fourth Chapter of *Pastores Dabo Vobis*, paragraph 35, we read, "Every Christian vocation finds its foundation in the gratuitous and prevenient choice made by the Father 'who has blessed us in Christ with every spiritual blessing in the heavenly places, even as he chose us in him before the foundation of the world, that we should be holy and blameless before him. He destined us in love to be his sons through Jesus Christ, according to the purpose of his will.' (Eph 1:3-5) Each vocation comes from God and is God's gift. However, it is never bestowed outside of or independently of the church."

The family of Joe and Pat Shea, of Hazelton, North Dakota, was very conscious of "The church." They had been taught by their Irish Catholic father and their strong convert mother that "The church" was their connection with Jesus Christ and the source of their spiritual lives.

James, affectionately known always as "Jim," being the oldest, was very aware of the part the church played in his life. Growing up as the first born, he had received a deep respect and love for his Catholic faith from the beginning. This respect and love only grew stronger as the years went by.

I first met Jim in the spring of 1992. He was finishing his junior year in high school, and we met at a confirmation ceremony in a neighboring mission parish where he was serving the Mass. I had heard of Jim Shea from others. Even in his early high school years,

Jim was active in Teens for Life and other "church" activities. He was recognized for his gift of oratory and that spring evening in 1992, Jim gave a spiritual reading at the end of the Mass, challenging his classmates who were being confirmed. I was impressed–so much so that I suggested that Jim come to see me sometime and we visit about his future.

It wasn't until March 20, 1993, that Jim and I met at the vocation office to share some thoughts and pursue some possibilities for his future. In the meantime, I had learned that Jim was, indeed, thinking about the priesthood as his vocation. In his busy, teenage life, he found time for prayer and serious reflection about God's plans for him and he told me of this at our meeting. At the same time, Jim continued to be very active in Teens for Life, both locally and on the national level. At the time he was education director for the state board in North Dakota and was in great demand as a speaker on pro life issues.

As serious as Jim was about his vocation, he wasn't quite ready for the seminary. He had received a number of scholarships for college and we decided together that it would be good for him to accept one of those scholarships, for at least the first two years. Jim and I kept in touch during those two years. My stack of memos from our visits is evidence of how well Jim communicates and keeps in touch. Jim began attending our seminarian gatherings and became acquainted with the students who were already in the seminary. He was impressed, and the tug at his heart became stronger.

In the midst of his busy academic life, Jim also found time to teach religious education classes and work with young people in a variety of ways. He found this challenging and helpful in his discernment process. Faithful in his prayer life and seeking the help of a spiritual director, Jim came to the conclusion that it was time for him to officially enter the seminary.

Like many young men considering a vocation to the priesthood, Jim was not certain about where God wanted him to be a priest. Was it the diocesan priesthood or a religious community? The summer of 1994 was a time of decision making. The struggle was real and the doubts and fears were daunting. Jim and I spent many hours together during that time of spiritual warfare, and there were times when it seemed that there was no sense of direction and no peace of mind or soul. It was a time of suffering–suffering which was both mental and spiritual, following closely upon the tragic death of Jim's youngest brother, Matthew, with whom Jim was very close.

The "daily cross" of which Jesus speaks in the Gospel, became very real for Jim. At the same time he discovered a deepening of his commitment to God's will and, finally, peace of mind along with the decision to enter the seminary the next year.

The Theological College of the Catholic University in Washington, D.C., offers a special scholarship to those who qualify, which includes expenses for three years of philosophy at their institution. It is called The Basselin Program, and Jim was interested. As a bright, intelligent young man, Jim had no problem qualifying for this special program. So, in August of 1995, Jim departed to spend three years at Catholic University and would graduate in the spring of 1998 with a master's degree in philosophy.

During his time there, Jim distinguished himself in a variety of ways. Always very personable and outgoing, Jim became involved with campus ministry at the University and found himself directing and giving retreats, teaching religious education, monitoring religious discussions and becoming involved in many other programs and activities.

Jim has an infectious personality. People like him and he is easy to like. He has many friends and they are true and genuine because that is the way Jim is. He is generous and kind-- always seeking ways to help and be of assistance to others. He amazes everyone with his energy and vitality and the ease with which he is able to accomplish so much. His leadership qualities and gifts are quickly apparent to those who meet Jim.

As the oldest in his family of seven boys and one little sister, Jim has learned to take the lead and do so with vigor and he does it well. After meeting Jim, one is not surprised that God has chosen him for service in the church. God has been good to Jim. He has blessed him with many gifts and Jim humbly knows this and understands something of the mystery of it all.

It has been a different journey for Jim Shea. It began with some uncertainty after several years of wondering, praying and seeking direction. The struggles have been real. The "moment of grace" just did not seem to come. Then the "light appeared," options began to focus, the grace of surrender was there and a generous response was given. The result is now a solid commitment to Christ and his church, both of whom are deeply loved and cherished.

Jim's vocation is strong. He is now in his second year of theology at the North American College in Rome. In just a little over a year, he has already been recognized for his leadership ability by his peers. They have elected him president of their class of 56 students. Jim will not disappoint them. Nor will he disappoint his God to whom he has given his heart and his life. It will be a few more years before the "grace of holy orders" is received from Christ through his church, but Jim Shea will be ready. He will be able to offer to the service of God's people a dedicated and blessed priestly ministry and the church will be richer for it.

Jim's Story...In His Own Words....

My father, Joseph Shea, was born and raised near Hazelton, North Dakota. He is the eldest of eight children. Grandpa Shea was a farmer and died while Dad was a sophomore in a high school seminary. Following this, Dad returned home to help with the family. My mother, Patricia Alpert, was raised in Richardton, North Dakota. Grandpa Alpert owned and operated a general store. Mom is the sixth of seven children and a convert to the Catholic faith.

On March 27, 1975, three months after my parents' first anniversary, I was born at St. Alexius Medical Center in Bismarck, North Dakota. Soon after this, we moved onto the Shea family farm two miles north of Hazelton, a town located southeast of Bismarck with a population of about 250. Agriculture is the main industry there, and I grew up surrounded by the hard-working, down-to-earth atmosphere of the small family farm. Dad wanted me to assist him with the farm work from an early age, and I still remember raking alfalfa when I was in the second grade. It was the first time I operated a tractor. I also learned to milk cows when I was very young.

The eighteen years I lived on the farm taught me the value of hard work and a love for the land, even though I never brought myself to love the hard work. I realize now that growing up in that wholesome environment did much to form me into who I am today.

From those first years of life to the present day, the church has always had a strong presence in my life. The devotions of my aunts, uncles, grandparents, and parents greatly impressed me as a young boy, and I do not remember a time when Catholicism was not an element of my identity, a defining characteristic of who I see myself as. A combination of my family's dedication to the church, a strong parish community at St. Paul's in Hazelton, and the dedicated ministry of the Precious Blood Fathers, who served the parish for most of my youth, prompted me to consider the priesthood from an early age.

Sorting through the earliest memories of my childhood, I notice the faded image of a church interior, statues, flowers, candles, stained-glass, incense, and a priest at the altar, praying. The priest is Father Bill Dougherty, a Precious Blood Father and pastor at my home parish. That quiet drama of the Mass, played out week after week some twenty years ago, made a deep and lasting impression upon me. To a little boy from the farm two miles up the road, here was a mystery and beauty different from the rest of life. As tough as it is to figure out just how God works in our hearts, I suspect that those moments were the first seeds of my vocation.

There are other memories, too: the family rosary, prayed in the living room before bedtime or in the van on any trip of 15 miles or more; kneeling with my mom late into the night at adoration on Holy Thursday; watching my dad drop to his knees in the earth to pray after the last round of spring planting. These and so many other little things shaped me , and it was in them that I first heard the call of God in my life. At the time I suppose they all seemed very ordinary. But those little things had what it took, because I know I didn't find my vocation in the high drama of a single moment. I heard the call of Christ in his gentle, abiding presence--in my family and through the church.

I don't recall just when the idea of a vocation to the priesthood first occurred to me. At least up until second grade I was pretty certain that I wanted to be a policeman. But I was wavering on that soon after my First Communion, and before long I was confident that I would be a priest. I don't remember the exact details well because the idea of the priesthood never struck me as strange or out-of-the-ordinary. My dad and several of my uncles had been in the seminary. Why not give it a shot?

But sooner or later junior high school came along. Those were difficult years, and along the way I mostly forgot about becoming a priest. It wasn't until my sophomore year in high school that I began to think seriously about the priesthood again. And that wasn't an accident, either. It was about then that I began to go to confession regularly, and I found a great deal of comfort and relief in the sacrament. Before long, I was going every week. It really affected me to realize that there was another person to whom I could take everything, not only the nightmares of sin but the little joys and sorrows of everyday life I could pour out all of my worries, concerns, triumphs, sins, failures, and progress. I could ask for advice and receive practical, concrete guidance. Confession became in many

159

ways, the well-spring of my vocation, the fortification of my faith life, and the instrument that Christ used at that time to warm my heart with his love.

So it was in that discovery that I first began to think about the priesthood as a practical reality. If the church would take me, if I could make it through, I wanted to be there like my pastor was there for me. Sure, I wanted to be with people in the big turning points--to marry their children, to bury their dead. But more than anything I just wanted to be there for them in life itself, with all of its ups and downs.

I first went to speak with Msgr. Gerald Walsh, vocation director for the diocese, in the spring of my senior year in high school. It was the first of many visits. We talked about possibilities for the future and about the nature of a priestly vocation. I vividly remember two things from that first visit. First, Monsignor gave me a copy of *Pastores Dabo Vobis*, the Holy Father's exhortation on the formation of priests, which at the time was less than a year old. Second, while we were chatting about scholarships and academic formation, he mentioned a scholarship program at the Catholic University of America in Washington, D. C. for the study of philosophy. He offered to check into it, and I remember telling him something like, "Well, look into it if you like, but don't waste too much time. I don't think I am interested.

As intent as I was at that time about giving the seminary a shot, I didn't feel any particular urgency about the matter. In the end, I accepted a full scholarship at Jamestown College, just a hundred miles from home. I was to remain there for two years.

I was delighted by what I discovered at Jamestown College. The classes were challenging, rigorous, and personal. I found the professors brilliant and full of love for learning. College life enchanted me, and I delved into it wholeheartedly. In addition, I must attribute to Jamestown College an immense strengthening of my faith. Because the majority of students who study religion and philosophy there are Protestant, I was forced to study my Catholic faith more closely in order to articulate it at all. And the lessons I learned about friendship and fellowship there with them will stay with me for the rest of my life.

My youngest brother, Matthew, was killed in a sledding accident on March 1, 1994, during my first year at Jamestown. He was one of the most precious people in my life, and the loss was devastating. Burying my brother was very difficult, and it was a struggle to see God's will in the following months. But the faith that God has prepared me and my family with sustained us through that time. It helped us to recognize how this tragedy strengthened our family and even deepened our faith by showing us how much we depend upon God. I was startled by the support offered by the church during those long weeks. Bishop John Kinney visited our family during the day of the vigil and seven priests, including Msgr. Walsh, concelebrated the Funeral Mass the following day. Sister Michaeleen Jantzer, the pastoral minister at St. James in Jamestown, spent several days with the family. The great compassion of the church and the power of Christ's ministry during that time deepened my love for the church and my attraction to the priesthood as never before. Looking back now I also see how Matthew's death brought my priorities into sharp focus. The gravity and pain simply crowded out old distractions and hesitations and made me eager for a radical change.

That summer I departed by Cheshire, Connecticut, to enter the candidacy program for the Legionnaires of Christ. It was a summer of great blessing and great struggle, all at the same time. There were sixty young men in the program, all eager to give their lives to Christ. I had never before been in an environment with so many other young men enthusiastic about their faith. Being away for a bit with a lot of new people also helped me to quietly grieve the loss of my brother, and it was a time of incredible healing. But it was also a very difficult time, because the difference between the life of a diocesan parish priest and a priest in a religious community became clear to me for the first time. I had no idea where God wanted me, or even to which I was more attracted. Despite the advice of both Msgr. Walsh and my superiors in Cheshire, I became almost frantic about the matter. My prayers for guidance were absorbed with panic and quiet desperation.

But at least when the end of the summer arrived, it was clear to me that I wasn't ready for the novitiate. As I packed my things, my superiors told me, "You're always welcome to come back if you like, but it's probably a good idea to give Msgr. Walsh a call without wasting too much time." So I flew back to Jamestown to begin my second and final year at Jamestown College. I think my parents and Msgr. were all glad to see me home again.

As happy as I was to be back at Jamestown, I began to realize during the course of the year that I wouldn't be able to remain there. I finally felt ready to enter the seminary, and I knew deep down that it was time to move along. But I also knew that leaving Jamestown in mid-stride would be very difficult. I suppose I was most afraid of leaving so many close friends behind. It wouldn't be like graduation, with each person going his own way. Rather, I'd be stepping out of the circle, leaving a life that would go on without me. But my friends were understanding and supportive, and I began to prepare myself for the big change.

In the spring of 1995 I was offered the Basselin Scholarship at Catholic University, the same program Msgr. Walsh had mentioned to me on our first visit. Ironically, the program is geared to accept candidates who have completed two years of undergraduate study elsewhere, so our timing was perfect. I was nervous, though, both about entering the seminary, and also about moving to a big city on the East Coast. In order to earn a little extra spending money, I spent the summer in Jamestown working as assistant director public relations at the college during the day and at McDonald's in the evenings. At the end of the summer I boarded a plane for Washington, D.C.

Basselin Scholars live at the Theological College, the University seminary, and engage in three years of intensive philosophical study and research. At first I found the academic demands almost impossible, and I particularly remember agonizing for hours over a branch of philosophy called metaphysics, characterized at Catholic U. by the study of the works of St. Thomas Aquinas. But pretty soon I caught on, and I even began to enjoy the rigor and challenges of the program.

But I didn't study all of the time at Catholic U. I was active in campus ministry and also student government; in both places I had fun and learned an awful lot. I taught religious education in some of Washington's toughest inner-city schools and worked with Mother Teresa's sisters at a shelter for the homeless with AIDS. In addition to directing pro-life activities at the seminary, I got as involved as I was able in other aspects of campus and seminary life. But more than all of that, I made good friends during those full and joyful years, and I came to love Washington and Catholic University. Nevertheless, by the spring of 1998 I was ready for graduation and for moving on to the study of theology and the final four years of seminary training.

I had a few precious weeks with my family back in North Dakota before leaving to begin theological studies at the North American College in Rome. On June 30, I received Candidacy from Bishop Paul Zipfel in his chapel. It was the first official step towards priesthood and my whole family was there with me. Msgr. Walsh was there, too. It was his last day as diocesan vocation director (he retired the next day on July 1), and I was deeply moved as I thought about how much he had seen me through. By and large, I know that it was Msgr.'s gentle and persistent guidance that saw my childhood notion of the priesthood turn into a concrete plan of action.

You know, there's a point where gratitude is too much for words. I suppose all we can do then is take what we've been given and give thanks with our lives. I pray that, if I make it to ordination, I might be a priest like Msgr. Walsh and Fr. Dougherty and the many other happy and holy priests who have touched my life. It's something else to help another person better hear the call of God in his heart, and they did that for me. Laboring for the Kingdom of God, I'm told, is reward enough in itself.

TWENTY

Christopher Kuhn
As I Recall Him

It is easy for a family of 5 or 10 or 15 children to give one or more to the priesthood or religious life. When there is only one child, it is not so easy. Chris Kuhn is an only child. It didn't begin that way. There were three sons in the family of Rodney and Dorothy Kuhn. They lived in the country and were a happy family. Tragedy struck this happy family very early when two of the sons were taken—one by leukemia and the other through an accident on the farm. Not long after, the father suffered a series of strokes and did not recover. Chris and his mother remained.

When I first met Chris he was still in high school. A good student, serious and pensive, he was a young man who had known pain and loss and who had to grow up very quickly. Chris was very close to his mother and concerned about her having to work so hard to support him. He was and is a good son.

And in the midst of all this, he felt a tug at his heart towards priesthood. The Lord was quietly working in Chris' life. In his prayers, in his Mass serving, even in his loneliness, Chris felt drawn to something. He was not sure what or who it was. He began asking questions.

Chris became acquainted with some of our seminarians and attended several of our seminarian gatherings. He asked the right questions and became friends with the men in the seminary. By now he had graduated from high school and was attending the local junior college. At the same time he kept in touch and we first visited seriously about his vocation in April of 1996. Chris was beginning to feel very drawn to the priesthood. At the same time, as an only son, he felt responsible for his mother. He did not know how she would react to his interest in becoming a priest. He was, and is, a very responsible young man, mature for his age and serious about life.

At this time, Chris, thought that he should finish his two years of college at home and then enter the seminary in the fall of 1997 in his third year of college. Chris kept his promise. The moment of grace had come. He began to work on his application and soon was ready for the seminary.

He has completed his second year at the seminary and graduated with a degree in philosophy in the spring of 1999. He has entered theology at St. Paul Seminary in St. Paul, Minnesota, and will be ordained in four more years.

It has not been an easy decision for Chris. His best friend entered the seminary with him and then decided that this was not his calling and left. Chris has continued on, prayerfully responding to God's will for him, still concerned about his mother and growing in his wisdom and maturity every day. He is a reliable young man and will do what God wants him to do. He will find the right way and he knows now that his mother fully supports him in his vocation. He is at peace. He works hard during the summer months to finance his college. He has no other income. The child of single parent, he understands what he must do and does it.

Chris will bring many gifts to the priesthood. The Lord has tested him and Chris has responded. He knows what life is about–its sadness, pain and loss. He also knows of joy, victory and happiness and where they come from. Chris will be a patient and caring priest–understanding the crosses that people bear and walking with them in their pain. He will lift them up to the Lord in his own special way, and help them find comfort and peace, as he has done. His journey continues day by day and he walks it with confidence and joy.

Chris' Story...In His Own Words....

I want to begin by praising Jesus for his many gifts. It is for him that I write this story. I only hope that it gives him glory.

One of the most difficult questions for most seminarians is identifying that moment when the idea of priesthood really took hold. To describe the whole process of discerning a vocation usually is vague and uneventful. Maybe a couple of individuals have some flashes of clarity or some moving experiences about God's plan for them. Yet, most of us simply sail along and hope that the slight breeze pushes us in the right direction–a breeze that seems arbitrary at times, until after time goes by we can look back and see the course which was clearly charted for each of us.

I was born on December 8, 1976, in Bismarck, North Dakota. I often point out to individuals who know their feast days that there is a contradiction between my birth and the day we celebrate as the Immaculate Conception. By no means do I come close to being "immaculate."

Later, when I was a senior in high school my mother became more aware of my vocation. One night when we were sitting visiting about life--something we do occasionally--she told me about my father, the prophet. "This will be my priest," my father said, as he held me, his infant son back in 1976. This is a " prophecy" that burns in my mind every time I remember it. Little did my father realize what Our Lord was going to ask of him.

Not long ago, someone asked me a very interesting question–a question which really made me think. "Do you always introduce yourself as an only child?" "Yes, for the most part," I replied. This was the first time anyone had asked why I didn't mention my siblings.

It was a simple question with such a difficult answer. Why is it that I don't tell people that I am the second of three children? Maybe it is because I don't want sympathy, or maybe things are just easier that way, because my family does have a very interesting life–a life spent constantly in the presence and awareness of Our Lord, Jesus Christ. Jesus has always been with us so closely, only in a way that most people fear--in suffering and in death.

When I was about five years old my parents, Rodney and Dorothy, along with my two brothers, James, Lonnie and I, moved south of Bismarck onto a little "hobby farm." It was a "fixer upper" place with all kinds of interesting things for us boys to do. I still remember my brothers and I trying to catch mice in little styrofoam cups, and having to use a bucket outside for the restroom.

Naturally, we boys loved it in the country, and the location near the river prompted my parents to open a bait shop. The Last Chance Bait Shop it was called. The business was a slight burden on my parents who still maintained jobs in Bismarck. Mom was a nurse at St. Alexius Hospital, and my father was a guard at the State Penitentiary.

My brothers and I learned to fish, hunt and ride horses–everything boys should learn and experience. The gopher population took a sharp decline around the area, and my brother, James, and I became quite known for our fishing skills. I mention James because Lonnie wasn't with us very long. Lonnie was my younger brother, born on April 30, 1978. He was a brother who had the face of an angel. That is how I always remember his face when I try to picture him, not blue and lifeless. Jesus has a plan for each of us and some people just don't get to play the game very long. Jesus had a short plan for my brother Lonnie–one in which Lonnie is my hero.

He saved my life that day. It was September 8, 1982. Lonnie was just four years old. I remember the day as sunny, warm and windy, and we boys were outside playing around the house. Mom was at work and Dad was trying to catch up on some sleep. He was usually behind because of our bait shop and his job as a guard. That day I was playing around all of the old appliances we had taken out of our home. There were lots of interesting things for us kids to play in. One thing that we played in was an old refrigerator, the kind that doesn't open from the inside.

As I began playing in that old refrigerator, I became terrified as I realized that the wind had shut the door on me. It was very dark and the air around me became very cool. I began to panic and to shout. It was then that he saved me. All of a sudden there was bright sunshine and my little brother's angelic face. It is the last living image of his face that I remember. The next time I saw his face it was cold and blue for that was the same day and in the same refrigerator that Lonnie died. Later in the day, Lonnie thought it was fun to play in that refrigerator as I had done but no one found him until it was too late and he suffocated.

My father never really forgave himself for having left that refrigerator around. My mother says he felt responsible for Lonnie's death, a responsibility that put a lot of stress and anxiety on my father. It was an added burden that proved to be too much. As a child my father had suffered from rheumatic fever, a condition that weakens the heart permanently. I'm no doctor but I think that condition had something to do with his strokes later on.

Sometime after this, James, who was born September 21, 1973, became sick with cancer. He had leukemia, a common form of cancer for children. The actual dates I don't remember. I am sure that my mom remembers, but I never was a detail guy. What I do remember is the ride home with Mom from Victor and Mary Richter's farm. The Richters were and are a traditional Catholic family who lived about eight miles from our place. Mary and Victor have fourteen children, thus James and I were able to find at least one of them who was close to our ages. James' best friend in the Richter family was Patrick and mine was Jerry Richter. We four boys were very close, and as time went on the Richters became family to me. That family will never know how important they are to me. Where God takes away, he gives back so much more.

Riding back with Mom, she began to explain to me what was happening to James. This was something very difficult for a parent to explain and for a child to understand. What I did know was that things were not good. I faintly remember going to school shortly after that and realizing just how sad things were. I can't describe my thought, but I was struck with a profound sense of fear and sorrow. I began crying at recess, and I remember sitting on the steps of the school in tears. God became more real that day. From that point on I remember praying to him often.

James was ill for about three years, although, during the first year after his diagnosis he went into remission and he was doing well. We spent almost every day fishing together and hunting. Oh, and the fighting! We used to fight like crazy. The fights ranged from fists to BB guns. Although I never really won any of those fights, James left me with the illusion that I had. I would usually start crying and then, so as to get me to be quiet and not tell how he had tormented me, he would let me get in a few good swings. This was followed by his act where he pretended to have been hurt worse than I was. Those big brothers are really a pain. I remember when he used to fake injuries out in the middle of nowhere and tell me to go for help. Naturally, I would run off screaming, terrified that he was really hurt. He was "the king of acting," always looking for attention.

During this time my father suffered his first stroke. He was very young for such a devastating health problem. Paralyzed on his right side and mentally changed forever, he became in many ways a stranger. After that my father could hardly speak, unless you consider swear words to be an effective form of communication. Don't get me wrong, he wasn't overly abusive outside of the fact that we felt like we needed to "walk on egg shells" around him. He was still a good man at heart, but he was so angry inside and very frustrated with his

170

debilitated condition. He was able to walk, but not well. He struggled to do things which he enjoyed and which before had been so easy. And there was still this passion for coon hunting and coon dogs. And that stupid mule!

Hunting in the river bottoms for raccoons required three things: a gun, dogs and a mule. He had a mule that was the epitome of mules. It scared my mom when Dad went out hunting, given his physical state, yet he always made it back safely. Sometimes, though, the mule made it back before he did, or he would return without the mule. I can only imagine what those nights were like for him.

And the dogs! The dogs were just as difficult. I remember one time when one of the dogs took off on him. The next day Dad was so mad. The dog was gone. Instead of raccoons, he was out hunting the dog. I was with him and when he found him, he took about five shots at the dog from about four hundred yards. Lucky for both of them, Dad wasn't shooting very good anymore. I say lucky for Dad because he really loved his dogs. Eventually, the dog returned home when it became hungry and Dad accepted him back with a slurred smile.

Needless to say, my mother was struggling to hold our shattered family life together. She was originally a rather submissive person. Dad was the leader. All changed, however, after Dad had his stroke and James was ill. She was forced to become the mother of us all. She rose to the occasion, regardless of her own personal need for security and support. She became the nurse for our family. She must have been so scared. I don't think there are but a few people who experience the worries and problems that she had. I am convinced that it was only through the grace of God that she was able to do what she did. She had pressures and responsibilities only Our Lord could share.

There is absolutely no way that I can ever understand the depth of this woman's heart and will. When life lets you down, try meditating on her life for a little while. A man that she loved so passionately and so deeply was no longer there (alive, but changed). One of her children had died in a tragic accident while another son's life hung in the balance. My mom worked hard and was forced to unwillingly accept the worst that life had to offer. Tragedy after tragedy. When James came out of remission, there wasn't much time left, and the time that he had left he chose to endure without medication. He was tired of fighting and was ready to submit. He spent the last few weeks of his life lying on our living room floor. We brought a mattress down from upstairs for him. This way he could still be with us throughout the day, instead of up in his room. What do I remember most? The crushed ice. James was so weak that he could barely lift himself up into a sitting position on the floor. He was so weak that walking wasn't an option. My greatest service to him was getting crushed ice for his thirst. He was always so thirty and his lips were so dry and cracked.

Finally, the day came when he died. He knew it was coming and we took him to the hospital, stopping at Richter's on the way to get some water. That night we watched him slip into a sleep from which he would never awake, a sleep which stopped with our good-byes. I still remember my mother calling me over to his side to say good-bye to him. I still remember that peaceful expression on his young face. It is one of my most cherished memories. Being there at his death was a beautiful gift. Thank you, Jesus.

I wasn't very thankful for quite some time afterwards. I felt cheated and angry at God. I still remember driving around on James' four-wheeler, which he had received from the Make-A-Wish-Foundation. I cursed God that day with a degree of anger that I have never felt since in my life. But then, life seemed so unfair. It wasn't until about two years ago that I was able to apologize to God and ask for forgiveness during confession. My anger was long gone, but I had never really made an apology to Our Lord. Those stages of grief are easily seen now as I look back on my life.

When my father died on June 8, 1993, he was forty-five years old. It was the third stroke that eventually took his life–a blessing in the end. After his second stroke things had only become worse. I can recall it as though it was only yesterday. It is a strange coincidence that I was present at all of those events. Dad's second stroke became too much for my mother and for me. Two weeks before my freshman year at St. Mary's High School, we moved into Bismarck and eventually had to put Dad into a nursing home.

My mom was mentally and physically drained and, to be honest, so was I. It was a very difficult thing for my mother. But she did the right thing. My father was so difficult to care for that he was moved from one home to another. Eventually, he ended up at the Kensington Apartments in Bismarck. There he was pretty much on his own, surrounded by Alzheimer patients for the most part. He was irritated by his neighbors, but more independent and uncrowded.

I visited him at least once a week, and he came home sometimes with Mother for the day. It was so sad. I remember the last visit with him sitting in silence for the most part and telling him that I was thinking about the seminary. He clasped his scapular and mumbled some things to me that I couldn't understand. Jesus became alive to him eventually in his sufferings. He was no saint throughout his life, but I like to think that he did more than enough penance at the end.

When he died, Mother and I hugged one another and cried as we stood by his lifeless body that night. As I hugged her and sobbed, I looked at him on the floor and cried not so much for him but for the father I never really knew. Then I felt happiness for him because at last he was finally free. Thank you, Jesus.

How does all of this relate to my vocation story? This is what has brought me to where I am now. The constant struggle for life and its sufferings in my family has forced me to look for answers. There comes a point in our lives when we have to decide on issues like the existence of God, and try to explain the reality we live in. Either life is arbitrary and meaningless or orientated towards something.

For me, my heart has struggled with such issues and I can't deny that there is something more than this world, and that this

173

'something' is guiding me towards a goal. I wish I could explain to you with reason what is in my heart, but that would deny the importance of faith. There is a God and he calls each of us through the circumstances of our lives to become his servants. He gently makes us into what he wants us to be, and sometimes some of us need to experience him in more profound ways. I believe that is what my life has been about.

On that night when Mom told me what my Dad had said, "This will be my priest," I told her that I wouldn't want my life any other way. It was this gift of life and death that has made me into who I am. My "prophetic" father had no idea what his wish for me would entail. Through it all, Jesus became a deeper friend and source of comfort for me—something I believe I would have never experienced otherwise.

Do I have a genuine priestly vocation? I don't know for sure. That is why I am in the seminary. But what I do know is that Jesus has directed me here. And because he has given me so much, I strive to return what I can. A constant desire for service and the question of his will for me keeps me here.

"Will you be my priest?" We don't always see the course that Our Lord has chartered for us, the ways in which he calls us to his service. All we can see is the past, and estimate our destination. Like a ship blown by the wind, we travel through life. But rest assured, Jesus is at the wheel, and he knows where we are heading.

TWENTY-ONE

Keven Wanner
As I Recall Him

I have found over the years that brothers often play a very great part in the whole vocation picture. Before I met Keven Wanner, I had been visiting with one of his older brothers about a possible vocation to the priesthood. We had several meetings and some good serious discussions. At the same time, the struggle between the vocation of priesthood and marriage were very real in this young man's life and at the end we agreed that marriage was his vocation.

In the meantime, I had received a letter from Keven in September of 1994 in which he expressed an interest in seminary life and priesthood. Keven had attended a "live-in weekend" at the seminary and had been impressed with what he experienced. Keven was still in high school at that time. He was a popular young man, very involved in sports, music and many other extra-curricular activities. He was looking forward to graduation and was becoming concerned about where he should go to college. These were all good and valid concerns of a devout Catholic high school senior.

I had not yet met Keven's parents but I knew that when two sons in a family of nine children are brave enough to express their interest in priesthood, the home life must be excellent. I was right. The family of Jim and Jean Wanner is the right kind of family from which priests and religious come. Dedicated to their Catholic faith and living that faith every day, Jim and Jean and their children are all involved in their small rural parish in a variety of ways. It's a perfect atmosphere for a vocation to priesthood to blossom and flourish.

As we finished our meeting that day, Keven promised to continue to pray about his future and be open to the voice of Christ as it would come to him in the quiet moments of his life. He also continued to be active in parish and school activities. He was a very bright and talented young man and a friend to everyone.

On Thursday, March 23, 1995, Keven came to see me at the vocation office. The tug at his heart was becoming stronger and stronger. It was Lent and during those days of grace, Keven had come to know Jesus in new and exciting ways. The "moment of grace" had come. He was ready to begin the journey. He was quite certain that the Lord was calling him to be a priest. He took an application and the process of entering the seminary had begun.

The memo I wrote on that occasion includes the following paragraph: "Keven's prayer life seems to be strong and he comes from a very good, solid Catholic background. He is the second youngest of nine children and seems to be very close to his family. He has been an altar boy for many years and continues to assist his pastor in many ways. Keven is a very good prospect and I promised to keep him in my prayers."

That following September found Keven enrolled in his first year of college at Cardinal Muench Seminary in Fargo. He soon proved himself to be a good student, bright and efficient. He was content in his decision and felt comfortable in the knowledge that he was where God wanted him to be. His determination was to prepare himself in the best possible way for priesthood and he set out to do just that. He has been faithful and dedicated in his spiritual life and also his academic life.

Keven has distinguished himself in many ways in the seminary and is highly respected and admired by his peers. They elected him to be president of the student body during his third year of college. This honor is usually given to someone in their fourth year of college. This is an indication of the impression which Keven has made on those with whom he lived and worked in the seminary.

Keven graduated from Cardinal Muench in the spring of 1999. He recently began his theology studies at the North American College in Rome. In the meantime, Keven has never forgotten where he comes from. He loves the farm on which his family lives. He works hard there during the summer months. And yet, he seldom misses daily Mass even when he is at home and the farm work is waiting. His parents graciously support him in this practice because they and Keven all know how important the Eucharist is in their lives and especially in the development of his vocation. His devotion is a quiet, steady devotion. His prayer is deep and persevering. Each year his vocation becomes stronger and his quiet yet outgoing personality expresses his peace of mind and contentment of soul in what he is doing.

Long convinced that a ready and sincere smile is a sign of God's presence in one's life, I often stress the importance of a large smile to the seminarians. Keven did not need to be reminded of this need. His smile is infectious and attractive. It speaks of an open heart and a caring soul, eager to reach out, to listen, to support and to help anyone who may be in need. The next four years will be interesting for Keven and for all who know him. If the last four have been any kind of an indication of what is to come, Keven will continue to grow and to blossom year by year.

And when the time comes, he will stand tall before the Lord and answer the church's call with a strong, convincing "I am here" when the moment of ordination arrives. His wonderful family, his many close friends, clergy and lay, his teachers and directors will all be able to say resoundingly, "I told you so." Keven Wanner will be an excellent priest!

Keven's Story...In His Own Words....

As I reflect upon my journey toward the priesthood, it becomes clearer in my mind how much God has blessed me over the years and how he has guided me onto my present course. It is not always easy to see how the Lord guides us according to his plans for us. That is why we must stop our hectic pace occasionally to look back on the ways God has directed our lives. It has truly been a great blessing to me to experience formation for holy orders. I am very grateful that God called me to the seminary where I could devote my attention to growing in my relationship with him and learning to prefer his will over my own.

Each vocation to the priesthood of Jesus Christ is a call to devote one's life entirely to the service of God and his people. It is an invitation to a special relationship with our Lord, one centered on love, service and a life of prayer. While in formation for priestly ministry, a seminarian has an opportunity for personal growth unlike any he has ever had before. He has the chance to be formed under the guidance of devoted souls, both clergy and lay, into the mature Christian we are called to be in Christ.

Priestly formation provides incredible opportunities for growth on both the spiritual and human levels. As a seminarian, I have been able to develop a deeper relationship with God through prayer and a new sensitivity to his will and the movements of the Holy Spirit in my life. I have a much deeper trust in the providence of God and a new confidence in the power of sacramental grace at work in the church. While in the seminary, I have grown in my understanding of myself and my relationships with others. I have learned how to better integrate my experiences, thoughts, and emotions so that I may become a healthier and more fulfilled person.

During my elementary years of education, I can't say that I felt any special vocation to the priesthood. Unlike some seminarians, I didn't feel a call to priesthood at an early age. I don't recall giving it very much thought at all at that point in my life, when I was far too involved in the everyday affairs of being a kid My only experience of the Catholic Church at that time was what I had encountered at my own small rural parish at Hebron, North Dakota. The only priest that I really knew was my own pastor, and even in his case, I can't say that he was a close, personal friend of mine. I knew very little about the life of a priest and the training that he must undergo before ordination.

No one, that I can remember, had ever asked me in a serious way to think about the priesthood. I never knew any seminarians nor had I ever seen a seminary or any Catholic school for that matter. Fortunately, although I had very little formal invitation to think about the priesthood, the conditions at home were good soil for God's seeds of a vocation.

My family had always been very important in my life and were very close to each other. Being second youngest of nine siblings, I always had the loving concern of brothers and sisters who were excellent role models for my formative years. My parents were always there to guide me toward a Christian life and the love of God.

Because I grew up on a farm/ranch, I learned to see the beauty in creation and the dignity of human labor, as we worked side by side as a family. Since I have come to the seminary, I have a new appreciation for the wonderful gift that my family has been to me. I cannot thank God enough for the graces he lavished upon me through them. I know that I would not be a seminarian were it for their example of Christian living and service to others.

In the summer of 1988, the summer before I began the sixth grade, an event transpired which shook my tidy, comfortable little world and changed my outlook on life. One of my older brothers was involved in a serious car accident resulting in a brain stem injury, which left him with what appear to be permanent injuries. The effect of this accident was devastating to my entire family and it left us asking the question, "Why us?" I was angry with God for quite awhile afterwards, that he could let this happen to us.

It was during the next several years that I really began to examine my life and to reflect on the bigger questions of life. After seeing how fast one's life can change, I began to ponder the meaning of life, the value of suffering, and the manner of God's love for us. In those years of suffering through my brother's slow and partial recovery, it was the grace of God that opened my eyes to a life of service to others in need. This was the time when God was speaking to my heart and calling me to himself, even though I couldn't recognize it yet.

During my junior high and high school years, my family was rebuilding and accepting the realization that my injured brother was not going to recover fully. My interest in the church began to grow during this period. I had been an altar boy for many years and was now serving as a lector, but I was compelled to think about higher forms of service than these. I began to see the need for priests in our diocese, as was clearly brought to my attention by the fact that my pastor had been in poor health for some time and no new priest had ever come to take his place.

I soon began to wonder about what kind of people became priests and what exactly it meant to be a priest. I had no concept of the extensive formation which seminarians undergo. I had never even seen a seminarian before. Although my interest in the priesthood grew, I didn't yet realize that I was called to that vocation. Actually, at that point I don't think the word "vocation" was part of my vocabulary yet. I had been well grounded in the modern mode of making a "career choice," which focuses completely on the self. Only as an awareness of God began to grow within me did I start to ask him what he wanted me to do in my life. Only then did I begin to ask for guidance in my decision making.

As my senior year of high school drew closer, I began to think more about career choices and where to go to college. I knew that I wanted to go to college, but I didn't have a clue about what I wanted to study. As I looked at my personal interests and skills, I couldn't help but think about the priesthood. I knew that I wanted a job where

I would be able to live a life of service to others and I felt that I possessed in some degree or another the skills that a priest might need.

Then one Sunday as I was leaving Mass, I saw a little pamphlet in the vestibule of my church that challenged me to think more about the priesthood. It was from Cardinal Muench Seminary in Fargo. After reading a few stories of the seminarians telling how they found fulfillment at the seminary, I found the courage to write a letter to the seminary asking for more information about what goes on there.

I was sent more information, primarily in the form of a priest from the seminary coming to supper at my house. I was amazed at the interest this priest had in me, and how much he was encouraging me to keep thinking about the possibility of priesthood. He invited me to come to the seminary for a live-in weekend, where I could see what goes on in the life of a seminarian and get to meet the other students. I thought it might be a good idea.

I had all sorts of pre-conceived notions as to what sort of a crowd these seminarians might be. First and foremost in my mind: they were undoubtedly going to be nerds. They would also have quite boring personalities, be out of touch with society, and have nearly identical interests. The vision I had in my mind was the bookworm type, whose favorite sport (if any) would certainly be chess.

I'm very glad that I went to that live-in weekend because I found out how dead wrong I was about the nature of seminarians. Here is the true picture. The students I met were by no means nerds, by no means boring, and by no means exact likenesses of each other. They were a very diverse crowd consisting of a range of ages and backgrounds. I discovered them to be very welcoming, friendly, and outgoing. They were funny too, but didn't need to offend Christian principles in being so, which was something very refreshing. That group seemed to care so much about one another, to be so happy to be there, and to be united for a common purpose: to grow in the love of God and to discern God's will for them.

I felt very much at home with them and longed for the inner peace which they seemed to possess. The great thing was that they could be all of this while at the same time being top-notch students. After playing a game of basketball with them, I could tell that chess was evidently lower than basketball on their list of favorite sports.

The priests at the seminary then informed the vocation director of the Bismarck Diocese, Msgr. Walsh, that I was interested in the priesthood. Monsignor has not been known to drag his feet when it comes to "reeling in" prospective seminarians. In my meetings with him, I became more excited about the priesthood. He seemed so happy to be a priest and was full of joy and love. I saw in him what I wanted to become. I now saw the possibility of being both very happy and a priest at the same time.

I decided that I had to give the seminary a try. I figured that coming right out of high school was the best time for me to enter. That way if the seminary was the place God wanted me to be, I wouldn't be wasting any time; if it wasn't, I could get on with my life. I felt that I had nothing to lose by spending a year in priestly formation. The experiences I would have there would be a great benefit to me, whether or not I would go on to become a priest.

At the time I entered, I remember feeling very good about starting my college career as a member of a close brotherhood. I knew that having good, virtuous friends, was important. These are the very types of friends one makes at a seminary. Seminarians genuinely care about each other and become very close because they are on the same spiritual walk, facing the same joys and fears together. The seminary community is really a family, a family united in charity and the common goal of becoming instruments in God's hands for his greater glory.

Being in a formation program for holy orders is like taking one, big course in spiritual conversion. The formation program has challenged me to grow in so many ways: spiritually, academically, emotionally, and physically. Sometimes it has been hard to keep moving toward the goal of molding myself into the person of Jesus Christ. He is such a high goal. Thankfully, he gives us sufficient grace to overcome the obstacles in our path. At many times over the past few years I felt that I would never make it, that I didn't measure up, that I would just never be holy enough to be a priest.

Now, however, I recognize Jesus telling me to put greater trust in him. I, of my own accord, can never be worthy to be a priest, but with the grace of God, I can be. If I wait until I am perfect to believe that God is accepting me as a seminarian, then I will always be let down. For it is God who is perfect, not us. We must come to him as we are, weak and sinful, so that he can uproot the evil in us and refashion us according to holiness.

This has been my biggest struggle while in the seminary, with my third year being the hardest. It took me several years to finally turn my life over to God more fully and trust in his grace to be sufficient for my weaknesses. It is not easy to give away control of our lives to someone else. What better person to give that control to than God himself? He knows our every need and desire. He knows what is best for us.

My greatest joy while in priestly formation has been experiencing the love of God, which I have felt in a variety of ways. I have felt the power of God's love when receiving the sacraments and participating in the liturgies of the church. I have seen his loving presence in the smiles and concerns of my brother seminarians. The guidance and instruction of priests and professors has also been a sign of God's love for me. The many faithful members of God's flock, who have given me so much prayer and support, are also an image to me of the love of God.

And how can I forget about my own family and friends? They have offered many prayers on my behalf and are so eager to see me become an ordained minister of God. God's love for me is all this and much more.

I no longer question the depth of God's love for me. In my heart I know that God has many beautiful plans in store for me, just as he does for all of his children. The realization that God is at work in my life has been for me a source of constant joy and hope. Even in the midst of all my sinfulness, inadequacies, trials and doubts, I have the sweet consolation of God's presence and the promise of his love to see me through them.

I have been called to the seminary to come to know the person of Jesus Christ and to model him in my own life. God has challenged me to enter into a closer relationship with him and to separate myself from worldly attachments which would hold me back. With the help of grace, I can continue to live up to that challenge. I pray that, if it is God's will, I may one day be able to reflect his immense love for his children as a priest, to love and serve as did Christ Our Lord.

TWENTY-TWO

Peter and Paul Eberle As I Recall Them

The well-known Serra International group includes a vocation program entitled "Called By Name." The National Conference of Catholic Bishops supports this program, among others, and promotes it in their vocation manual entitled *A Future Full of Hope*.

We have used this program with some consistency in our diocese and the following is the story of one success from "Called by Name."

It was in the fall 1993 that our diocesan vocation team conducted this program in one of our more Catholic counties–Emmons County in the southeast corner of our diocese. We covered six parishes that weekend and the members of those parishes recommended over 80 names of young men and about 20 names of young women whom they considered to be good candidates for priesthood or religious life.

Among the names were those of two brothers--twins--by the name of Peter and Paul Eberle. They were just sophomores in high school at that time but were altar servers and members of a devout Catholic family in the area. The family included 15 children. Peter and Paul were second youngest. With names like " Peter and Paul" they were natural candidates for priesthood, or so everyone thought.

When I contacted them after the weekend, they both agreed that they had thought about a vocation to the priesthood but they were quite young yet and were still praying about it. In February of 1994,

I interviewed them at one of the local rectories in the area and I was very impressed by their friendly sincerity and their questions. They were shy and respectful and their good Catholic family background was obvious. One could tell at a glance that they were used to sharing their lives with others. The "others" were their parents and 13 brothers and sisters at that time. They were very open and honest about their prayer lives and their religious training. They were curious and eager to learn more about vocations and priestly ministry in the church. They admitted that they were still thinking about the priesthood as their vocation. We parted with a promise to keep in touch and to pray for guidance. It would be three years before we would meet again.

On February 7, 1997, I wrote to them to see how things were going. It was a stroke of genius (and grace) because they were both getting ready to contact me about beginning the process of entering the seminary that fall. They had graduated from high school and were in their first year of college. The tug at their hearts had continued and the "moment of grace" was imminent. We met and visited and they convinced me that they were both ready to begin the journey. Christ was very real to them. Their vocations were strong.

Usually, I would question the motive of one or the other of two brothers who are twins or very close as Peter and Paul are, and who *both* want to enter the seminary. In this case, however, after interviewing them separately and confidentially, I was convinced that each of them was properly motivated and felt called to be priests. We began the process of application.

Peter and Paul have completed two years in the seminary. They are both happy and continue to grow, like the Child Jesus, "in wisdom, age and grace." When they arrived at the seminary for a visit before entering, the good rector, Father Brian Donahue, said to me, "These boys have priesthood written all over them. They never stop smiling!"

The discipline of being part of a family of 15 children, the hard work ethic which their farm background has taught them, and their natural good nature and generous hearts have made Peter and Paul outstanding candidates for priesthood. Each of them has special gifts, yet they share many of the same attributes and family values. They are sincere and devout. They are generous with their time and talents and look for ways to be of assistance to others.

They are close in their brotherly affection and concern for each other, and yet are not exclusive in their choice of friends. They are well liked and popular, good students, dedicated and faithful at prayer, and interested in others. They will tell you in their own individual stories just how different they are. It is not obvious to others. In fact, being identical twins has its pluses and minuses. It takes one awhile to be able to tell them apart. They are that much alike, both in good looks and demeanor.

Peter and Paul been blessed in many similar ways. At the same time, they express their own individual opinions, which often differ, and they insist on their individuality in many ways. They are not clones of each other. Each one has a unique vocation and a unique relationship with Christ, who has called them.

Peter and Paul, like their patron saints, have much in common. In addition to being blood brothers and twins, they both feel called by God to serve him and his people.

At this writing Peter is considering a life of service in some vocation other than priesthood. He plans to take some more time away from the seminary after this year to further discern where God wants him to be and what God wants him to do. Our prayers and support go with him. Paul's plan is to continue in the seminary, pursuing a priesthood vocation and a future life of priestly ministry in the church.

Wherever God calls each of them to serve, they will give totally of themselves. Like their patrons they have responded and surrendered to God's call with all their hearts. Their smiling faces and sincere care for others will serve them well in any ministry. They have much to give to God and his church and they are ready and anxious to do so. Theirs will be an interesting and a blessed future. They are young "apostles" in love with Christ ..... "Called by Name."

Peter's Story...In His Own Words....

The idea of being a priest came to me on occasion during my childhood, but I always thought, "I could never be a priest; I could never be that holy and do all the things a priest does." I can recall people from the community, my pastor and my parents telling me that they thought I would make a good priest and that I should give it some thought. Well, during those days I didn't give much thought about what God wanted me to do for the rest of my life. I was content with school, work, friends, and sports, and a decision about a vocation seemed an eternity away at the time. So when I was asked if I would want to be a priest I was content with just answering, "well...maybe." Consequently, I was challenged from a young age to consider the priesthood as a vocation to which God might be calling me.

There were many experiences in my life that spurred me to think about the priesthood more seriously. I will tell about one of these experiences that stands out most in my memory. At home one evening, when my brother Paul and I were sophomores in high school, we started to talk to each other about the feelings we had about a possible vocation to the priesthood. We both acknowledged that we had thought about the priesthood, but at the same time we couldn't fathom that it could be a reality. We didn't think we were worthy to be priests. We both decided to pray that we might know God's will for us. A few minutes after our conversation the phone rang. It was Monsignor Gerald Walsh, the vocation director for the diocese. He asked if Paul and I ever thought about the priesthood and said that he would like to visit with us about it sometime. As can be expected, I was very surprised and puzzled by this phone call and I remember thinking, "How could this be happening? Paul and I think about the priesthood but don't tell another person and now we get a call from the vocation director wanting to talk to us about the priesthood."

Monsignor Walsh went on to explain to me that the parishioners in my community had submitted our names when the "Called By Name" program took place in our parish on a Sunday a while back. The "Called by Name" program involved parishioners submitting names of people of the parish who they thought would make good candidates for the priesthood or religious life. On the phone, I told Monsignor Walsh that Paul and I had thought about the priesthood and we agreed to meet with him when he was going to be in the area. I truly believe that the Holy Spirit was at work that evening allowing things to turn out the way they did–if for no other reason than to let Paul and me know that we were on the right path by being open to a vocation and thinking about the priesthood, and planning to continue to pray about it. I was filled with a strong assurance that God was, in fact, guiding us.

Paul and I had a general idea about the priesthood from observing priests and reading some material, but we had really no idea what seminary training was like. Monsignor Walsh gave us a better understanding about what the seminary and priesthood were about. He gave us guidance as to how to identify signs that we might have a vocation to the priesthood. He expressed how very happy he was to be a priest and said that if God is calling us to be priests we would be very happy doing God's will. Monsignor's advice and encouragement inspired me to keep praying to know God's will for me.

After that visit, Monsignor occasionally sent Paul and me a seminarian newsletter entitled *The Chosen*. Receiving this letter was always a grace for me because it encouraged me to persist in prayer for guidance. I felt that it would only be fair to God and myself to leave myself open to a vocation to the priesthood. I knew I needed to give it thoughtful consideration.

During the next few years in high school my feelings about a possible vocation to the priesthood went back and forth. At times I thought, "yes, God is calling me to be a priest," and at other times I thought, "there is no way God is calling me to be a priest. I am too much of a sinner." I often felt unworthy to even consider it as an option, but God had provided me with many motivations to persist in being open to a vocation.

The desire to help others and live a holy life were my main motivations in high school to consider the priesthood. During my junior year of high school I thought about it frequently. I couldn't deny that nudging by God to consider the priesthood although I knew it would be a long time before I graduated and made a decision about further education.

In 1996 I graduated from high school and enrolled at the University of Mary in Bismarck that fall. I didn't have the courage to enter the seminary after high school, even though deep down I had really wanted to, but I attempted to put off the idea for awhile. During my second semester at the University of Mary I could not longer deny God nudging me to join the seminary. I finally decided to give the seminary a try along with my brother Paul who also felt called to the priesthood.

Before Paul and I got in touch with Monsignor Walsh to talk to him about wanting to join the seminary, he wrote us a letter asking us if we were still thinking about the priesthood and if we could visit with him sometime. In the following weeks we talked with Monsignor, visited Cardinal Muench Seminary in Fargo, and officially started the application process to enter the seminary. Paul and I began our studies at Cardinal Muench Seminary in the fall of 1997. I believe the Holy Spirit was answering my prayers for guidance by this gradual easing me into the seminary in this way. I felt very confident that I was making the right decision and was being led by God on the right path.

I will now give you an overview of important things in my life that contributed to my decision to enter the seminary. I grew up in a large Catholic family of 15 children–nine boys and six girls. Paul and I are twins and the second and third youngest respectively. I am eight minutes older than Paul. I grew up on a farm until I was about ten years old. My dad began to have heart problems and was no longer able to do the physical work and deal with the stress related farm work without endangering his life. Therefore, we moved into the small town of Hague, North Dakota, which was only three miles away from our farm.

This move into town, however, didn't really keep our family away from the farm. My dad still had the land and there were enough of us boys at home to help with the work. My dad died of a heart attack in June of 1997, just four months after Paul and I had decided to enter the seminary. My dad had supported me in my decision to enter the seminary as did the rest of my family. They have been a tremendous source of support and prayer for me. They are truly blessings from God.

Getting back to my high schools days--like most teens I struggled with my identity and peer pressure. I often felt that I was living two separate lives--my faith life and my school life. It was hard for me to be myself and express my beliefs and feelings in school. This was a constant struggle for me since in high school I was very shy and reserved. I was self-conscious about what others thought about me and this caused a great deal of anxiety. I lacked the self-confidence to express myself, stand up for what I believed, and incorporate my faith into my whole life. I knew that God not only wanted me to be faithful when it was easy, but also when it was hard; especially when it was hard.

Even though I was aware of this, I gave into all kinds of peer pressure to drink alcohol and get drunk just to be accepted by friends. These situations that I put myself into were the cause of many sins. It was at these times I felt the most hopeless about having a vocation to the priesthood because I didn't think I would ever be strong enough to change. I kept praying to God for the continued grace to be aware of my sins and for the strength to do good. I must admit, however, that there were times I didn't want to be aware of my sins in order to feel less guilty when I did sin. For example, I would sometimes pray less the day before a beer party. This was very wrong and I knew that I needed to change.

While I was still living, in a sense, these two different lives--one in which I could be myself when I was around people I could really trust, and another in which I felt I needed to take on a different attitude to be accepted--I was feeling a strong call to holiness and was aware that God wanted me to live out my faith and convictions in an external way by reaching out to others and sharing my true self with them. This call to holiness I was experiencing caused me to think that maybe the priesthood was the way God wanted me to live this out. I felt that by being a priest I could share myself with others and be able to help others on the journey to God.

I can say without a doubt that my time in the seminary has been a tremendous growing experience. I am growing in my love for God, for others, and in my faith, but I am also growing to a greater understanding of myself and what I am called by God to do. This understanding of myself has helped me realize the need to step back from the seminary at the end of this year and re-examine my call to priesthood. I need to be sure that I didn't enter the seminary to run away from the anxieties that I had in high school. I need to be sure that my motives to be a priest were to be a true servant of God by serving his people and not solely for my own benefit. These are the main reasons why I feel that I need to take time off from the seminary.

I am so thankful that God has led me to the seminary. I trust that God will continue to lead me on the right path in life. I pray for all those who are discerning a call to the priesthood or religious life that you, too, may be granted the strength and courage to do God's will.

Paul's Story...In His Own Words....

I have a memory of a certain Sunday morning Mass sometime in the fall of 1993. At the end of Mass, our parish priest, Father Leonard Eckroth, made an announcement about a "Called By Name" program that was meant to foster vocations to the priesthood or religious life as a brother or sister. Father asked the ushers to pass out slips of paper and pencils to the parishioners and then asked everyone to write down the names of any people in the parish that they felt might be good candidates for the priesthood or religious life. Apparently my name, as well as my twin brother's name, was listed by some of the parishioners who thought that we could make good priests. As a result, Msgr. Walsh, the vocation director of the Bismarck Diocese, called us on the phone one night and asked us if we had ever thought about the priesthood. He said he would like to meet with us.

I remember the night that Msgr. Walsh called us. Peter and I were sitting in the living room just talking. I don't remember what we had been talking about but in the midst of the conversation Peter asked me if I ever thought about being a priest. He asked it seriously and as if it were a possibility that I would decide to become one. Peter and I talked about it for awhile and promised each other that we would be open to the priesthood. However, at that time we felt it would be very unlikely that God would call us to be priests.

This was the first time that I remembered seriously discussing the priesthood as a possibility with anyone. There were times before that when people said I should think about becoming a priest, but I never took it to heart as I did the night Peter asked me about it.

Within a couple of minutes after Peter and I finished talking about the priesthood, the phone rang. It was Msgr. Walsh. He asked us if we had ever thought about the priesthood. He said that there were people in our community who thought that we would make good priests. Peter and I had entirely forgotten about the "Called by Name" program and never expected to get a phone call as a result of it. Peter told Monsignor that we had thought about the priesthood and we were willing to meet with him. Monsignor encouraged us to continue praying about the possibility of God calling us to the priesthood and we agreed to meet with him at the rectory in Strasburg at a later date where he would be substituting for our parish priest, Father Leonard Eckroth.

Monsignor's phone call strengthened me spiritually and convinced me to think more about the priesthood. Peter and I felt a great need to pray about it because we believed that the Holy Spirit was working in our midst that night.

Peter and I met with Monsignor Walsh a couple of weeks later and we had a nice conversation about how we felt about the priesthood. I told him that I was far from knowing if the priesthood was for me, but deep down I felt it was a possibility. Monsignor told us to keep praying about it and to follow our hearts. He gave us some reading material that proved to be a tremendous help for me while praying about the priesthood. One book was called, *Speak Lord, I Am Listening*, by Bishop Sylvester W. Treinen, and another called *A Religious Vocation: Is It For Me?* by Rev. Martin W. Pable, OFM Capuchin. These books helped me to identify my feelings and realize that the priesthood was a possibility for me.

Throughout high school, I was blessed to have my twin brother, Peter, to talk to about my feelings. He was the only person that I felt could truly understand me. We would often talk about our feelings about priesthood. It helped me to identify what I was truly feeling and how God was leading me. I never told anyone other than Peter my deepest feelings about the priesthood and I only told my mom, dad, a couple of brothers and Father Leonard, that I was considering the priesthood. I didn't tell most of my brothers and sisters until after I had thought about it for a long time because I didn't want to feel pressured by them.

Also, I never told many of my peers that I was considering the priesthood, until I had decided to join for sure. In fact, I was even worried about some of them finding out. For one thing, I wasn't confident with myself and I thought that if some of them knew that I was considering the priesthood they would ridicule me and cause me to lose heart. In other words, I didn't want to feel pressured to enter the seminary by those who would give me encouragement, nor did I want to feel pressured not to enter the seminary by those who would ridicule an aspiration to the priesthood.

After my visit with Monsignor Walsh, I felt comfortable with letting the thought of priesthood just set in my heart. I felt that it was something tremendously important that needed a lot of prayer and consideration. I knew that it would take a lot of courage and determination to study to be a priest and that it would have to come entirely from God's grace, because at that time of my life I didn't feel that I would have the courage to enter the seminary. However, I was a sophomore in high school and I knew that it would be at least two years yet before I would decide where to go to college and what to study there.

Throughout the rest of high school, thoughts toward priesthood seemed to fluctuate between being strong and being weak. The thoughts, however, always remained with me even though at times I didn't feel strongly drawn to them. The thoughts of priesthood stayed with me because of Monsignor Walsh's seminarian newsletter which he would send to Peter and to me from time to time with a letter encouraging us to continue to consider the priesthood.

Also, my parish priest, Father Eckroth, often told Peter and me that he thought we would make good priests and encouraged us to think about the priesthood. These reasons, along with the encouragement of my parents and a longing to do God's will, kept the thoughts of priesthood alive within me through high school.

During my senior year of high school the thought of priesthood continued to be strong at times and weak at times. When it came time to decide which college to attend and what field of study to pursue, I didn't feel confident enough to enter the seminary. Instead, I decided to go to the University of Mary in Bismarck to discern what field of study to enter.

It didn't take much time in college before I began to feel more independent, not only in lifestyle, but also in my way of thinking. I no longer felt that I needed to live up to other people's expectations of me. I realized that if I was going to be happy in what I was doing, I needed to let go of my pride and stop worrying so much about what others may think of me. The people that I felt pressured by to maintain a 'cool' but false image in high school were no longer as much of a factor in college. This helped me to find my own identity. I was becoming increasingly more confident in simply being myself. During my second semester at the University of Mary, the thought of priesthood became stronger than ever. The independence that I experienced in college helped me to look beyond the wall of my pride and fears and into a very real possibility of becoming a priest As the year went on and thoughts of future plans became more imminent, I could no longer ignore my desire to give the seminary a try. Peter was also in much the same situation that I was and also felt that he needed to give the seminary a try as well.

Before Peter and I called Monsignor Walsh to tell him about our desire to enter the seminary, we happened to receive a letter from him saying that he would like to meet with us. Peter and I met with him and said that we felt God was calling us to the priesthood. He suggested that we visit Cardinal Muench Seminary, a minor seminary in Fargo, which Peter and I agreed to do.

I remember being nervous, but excited, about going to visit Cardinal Muench Seminary. I had no idea what the seminary was going to be like, much less the seminarians and priests. I had never been to a seminary or known a seminarian and I didn't know many priests. I was wondering if the seminary was going to feel like the right place for me and if I would fit in with the seminarians.

As we entered Fargo and got closer to the seminary the excitement continued to build. We pulled up to the seminary and when we walked through the front doors, Father Brian Donahue, the rector, was right there to give us a friendly welcome. Not long after arriving, we met a few seminarians and were overwhelmed by how friendly and welcoming they all were. They made us feel very comfortable and were interested in us and how God had been working in our lives to bring us to the seminary to visit. Many of the seminarians told us how they decided to enter the seminary and how they felt God working in them. It was reassuring to know that many of them had the same feelings about their discernment of the priesthood that I was having.

That evening the Bismarck seminarians took Peter and me out for pizza and we had a great time. Their joy and enthusiasm about being in the seminary gave me a lot of hope for the future and confidence in my own decision to enter the seminary. Before my visit to the seminary I had no idea what the seminarians were going to be like, but they proved to be extremely friendly, caring and down to earth people.

During the next day of our visit, Father Donahue gave us a tour of North Dakota State University, where the seminarians take most of their college classes, and talked to us about the seminary program and the application process. That afternoon Peter and I left for home with a wonderful feeling of thankfulness that God had graced us during our visit. We talked about our seminary visit on the way home and we were both pleased with it and decided that we should talk to Monsignor Walsh about starting the application process. Monsignor was happy to hear that we had enjoyed our visit and that we had decided to apply for entrance. It was hard to believe that I finally decided to do this. I realized that God had brought me a long way and had gradually supplied me with the grace that I needed to begin my seminary journey.

There were three main reasons why it was hard for me to decide to join the seminary: 1) I thought I would like to be married someday; 2) I didn't think I was holy enough to be a priest; and 3) I didn't think I would be capable of leading liturgies and preaching. I will expand

197

on each one of these reasons and explain how I am striving to overcome these seeming impediments.

The first reason, to put it simply: I was attracted to girls and wanted to get married someday. I knew that a priest couldn't get married and therefore I didn't want to be a priest. I felt that getting married and raising children would be the natural thing for me to do. My positive and joyful experience of growing up in a large family of fifteen children with loving parents made me want to aspire to the same thing. The deep love that my parents had for each other and their children had a profound influence on me. It helped me to see the Holy Spirit working in a marriage and the fruit that a loving marriage can bear. This was a reason for me wanting to get married and raise a family.

During high school, my experience of dating seemed to support my aspiration to live a married life. I enjoyed dating and I thought I would like to be married some day. It wasn't until my experience of dating in college that I began to consider more seriously my plans for the future. As I began college and thought about what I was going to do for the rest of my life, thoughts about the priesthood became stronger and stronger within me. I wanted to do something that would make a difference in the lives of the people that I was around and those of the whole world. I couldn't help thinking that the priesthood is a life that would offer me the opportunity to do just that.

The second reason for not feeling drawn to the priesthood was because I didn't feel that I was or could ever be holy enough to be a priest. I held the holiness and celibacy of the priesthood in very high esteem and I felt it took a person much more extraordinary than myself to be a priest. I had the notion that a priest was perfect and that I had to be perfect in order to be a priest. I failed to understand that priests are human like everyone else and cannot become holy by themselves.

Throughout high school I had found myself often choosing to do things that went directly contrary to my conscience. Beginning as early as eighth grade I started giving in to the peer pressure to drink beer and get drunk. This type of behavior continued through high school and I eventually came to realize that these actions were forming my conscience in the wrong manner and I needed to change this about myself. This realization became clear later on in high school when I realized that I was no longer giving in to peer pressure, but instead I was becoming a course of peer pressure for others, especially my underclassmen who were beginning to go to beer parties as well. I noticed my actions being an encouragement for them to drink. I didn't want that to happen because deep down I knew it was wrong and certainly not God's will. I realized that going against my conscience did not at all help me, nor the people that I was around, become better people.

The positive side to all of this is that I learned many good lessons about the reality of life and human weakness. I also learned that each of us has a very real and definite influence on the lives of the people around us and it is up to each of us to decide how we will influence one another. It may be your positive influence on someone that may encourage them to answer a call to the priesthood or religious life. After all, if it were not for the positive influence dominating the negative influence in my life, I wouldn't be in the seminary now discerning a vocation to the priesthood.

The positive and powerful influence in my life that I am speaking of is God's gift of my parents, my twin brother Peter, and all of my brothers and sisters. If it wasn't for the good examples that my parents, brothers and sisters set for me, I may not have been able to identify the direction my life was going in high school or have had the moral sense to change.

My twin brother, Peter, who was there to help me through many struggles in life, was a great source of strength and courage for me. These people were the ones that had the upper hand in forming my conscience and their great example of living our Christian values had a major influence on me.

Another aspect of my life that had a strong influence on my conscience formation was the Catholic education that I received at St. Benedict's Grade School in Strasburg. I attended St. Ben's until it closed at the end of my fifth grade year. I believe that the teachers at St. Ben's instilled in me a deep seated love for God and others. They taught me to be kind and respectful towards others and to love God above all. This was during the time of my life when values formation was most crucial. My Catholic education is truly a grace and I am very thankful to God and those who taught me.

Another thing that I learned from my parents and brothers and sisters is that there is a need to pray and work together as a family in order to have harmony in the home. As a family we would often pray the rosary together in the evening before going to bed. This coming together to thank God and ask him for his continued blessings was a source of lasting spiritual strength. It helped me to place my trust in God and it deepened my faith and conviction that God was a very real and intimate part of my daily life.

The third reason was what I felt to be a very practical reason for not being drawn to the priesthood. I didn't feel that I would be capable of doing the things that a priest does, such as leading liturgies, preaching and ministering to all different kinds of people. Being the second youngest child of fifteen children, I was more used to following the leadership of older brothers and sisters rather than being a leader myself. However, looking at my situation in retrospect, I learned how to be a good leader by the example of older siblings and at the same time learned how to follow the leadership of others and cooperate with them.

The main thing that I felt was going to be difficult if I became a priest was preaching. Many times it is hard for me to explain something in a way that is clear to someone else. My vocabulary always seems inadequate to get across how I really feel about something. However, this possible obstacle has also been a source of grace rather than a hindrance. It has helped me to realize that I need to place my trust in God and let him work through me.

I have been at Cardinal Muench Seminary for two years now and it has truly been a spiritually fruitful experience. Although I have doubts at times about whether the priesthood is for me, overcoming these doubt has strengthened my conviction about what I feel God is calling me to do. The spiritual and formation direction which I receive at the seminary has helped me to learn more about myself and has helped me to keep my mind and heart focused on doing God's will. I feel that God will somehow let me know where he wants me to be. Right now I feel he wants me to be at Cardinal Muench Seminary. I am learning much about myself and my faith here at the seminary and am looking forward to learning even more. I feel that the philosophy courses at NDSU and the religion courses at the seminary have broadened my horizons and given me new insights. Most importantly, daily Mass and prayer with the seminary community have strengthened and sustained me through my seminary experience. It is for these reasons that I am hopeful and find joy in continuing in the seminary to follow God's call.

✤ TWENTY-THREE ✤

John Gardner
As I Recall Him

In the Gospel of Luke we read about the calling of the apostles by Jesus. He called them by name, individually. There was no question of whom he was calling. It was very clear. We also read that the youngest apostle was one of the first ones to see and recognize Jesus as the Messiah. His name was John.

The youngest of our present seminarians is also a man named John. He, too, we believe, has been called by name. His name is John Gardner. John is the youngest in age and also in his academic formation. He is in his third year of college. Yes, John has a ways to go. No matter. When one is focused and goal oriented the years fly by. Ask any priest. We all wonder where the years went. Oh, yes, at times, especially toward the end of our seminary years, we thought ordination would never come. But it did, and it is always worth waiting for.

John Gardner is a bright young man with a great personality and a contagious sense of humor. He comes by it honestly from his Irish father and his French-German mother. I knew his good parents long before John was born as one of seven children. In fact, I witnessed the marriage of Dan and Maureen Gardner. It was a beautiful wedding and they have a beautiful marriage. They both come from strong

Catholic backgrounds and have formed an even deeper family religious spirit in their home.

Several of the older boys have considered the priesthood as their vocation, with the full prayer and support of their parents. John's older brothers were in contact with me before John expressed his interest in priesthood. These older brothers, at least for now, have decided to pursue other avenues of interest. John, too, after graduating from high school, decided to try college first.

Like others who find it difficult to let go of dating and the free life of college days, John wanted to see "what it was like" out there before a formal commitment. It was his first time away from home. It was not what John had expected--or maybe it was. At any rate, before his first semester in college was over, John was in touch with the vocation office about entering the seminary at mid-term. He was not sure if he should try it as a member of the Vianney Program (that is always a safe beginning) or whether he should make formal application to be accepted as a seminarian for the diocese and start the journey.

John had a deep prayer life. He had served as an altar boy in his home parish for many years. He was also gifted musically and had played the organ in his home parish throughout high school. Was he ready to give himself to the Lord? The tug at his heart was strong. He was attracted to the priesthood and priestly ministry. He had all of the signs of a worthy candidate....serious yet with a good sense of humor, prayerful without being obsessed, sincere and yet able to enjoy a good time. The Lord won out and John entered the seminary in January of 1998.

He would be our youngest seminarian at that time. He continues to hold that distinction as he begins his third year of college and third year in the seminary.

Like the young John of the Gospel, John Gardner is a favorite of all of our seminarians. He is genuine in his dedication to his vocation and all that it demands, and yet has a carefree sense about him which appeals to others. He can be witty and yet deeply devout, depending on the situation at hand. He is dead serious about doing what God wants him to do. He is also open to the grace which enables him to do just that. He is popular and well liked. His good Catholic family home life has prepared him well for service in the church. He is generous and caring–good qualities for a future priest. Called by name, as the Apostle John was, John Gardner knows clearly who has called him and to what he has been called.

It will be interesting to see where the Lord leads John in the next few years. His own story, like this one at this time, is rather brief. It will be an interesting one though, and will become even more interesting as time goes by. John has a future. Just six more years and he will be a priest. With many prayers and much support, with his continued deep devotion to Mary, Our Blessed Mother, and with the supportive help of his loving family, John, the youngest of our present "apostles," like John of the Gospel, will remain close to Jesus to the last.

John's Story...In His Own Words....

RRRIIINNNNGGG!!!!!!!!!! "Will someone please get the phone? Hey, Jack, it's for you!"

So you want to know how my call began? This scenario may have been the very beginning of God's call for me. My name is John Paul Gardner, but my good friends call me Jack, thanks to my dad. When I was born, Dad insisted on calling me Jack and Mom would not allow her son to have a name not included in the realm of sainthood. Perhaps she thought that one day I would be bound for sainthood. My dad and mom finally agreed to the name John since nine months prior to my birth, Pope John Paul II was elected Supreme Pontiff of the Catholic Church. My parents tell me that it is very possible that I was actually conceived at the exact moment the Pope was elected. Perhaps someday we will know.

So I was born into this world, and like most of the events in my life, my parents were to blame. I was born number three in the family. I surely thought that life was going to be rough....that is until God allowed my parents six more children. Now life wasn't going to be as rough as it had first appeared because I was going to have dominion over two younger sisters and four younger brothers. God is good!

Growing up with such a wonderful family was one of God's greatest gifts to me; however, I did not realize it until later in life. Some of my fondest memories are those of family vacations. Whether we were driving to California, Illinois, Nebraska, Canada, or just out to the farm, it never failed. Half of the time was spent saying the rosary, the other half of the time was spent sitting between my older brother Bill and Dave who were either punching me in the arm or pinching me until I cried. I still like them though.

During one of the vacations to the Black Hills in South Dakota when I was about 13 years old, I remember going to a Sunday Mass. After Mass, Mom and Dad were talking without restraint, and the kids were running around uncontrollably (as usual). For no apparent reason a couple of my brothers and I were playing around Dad and he introduced us to the man he was speaking with. Then the man looked at all of us at once with a smile, and he pointed his long shabby finger at me and said to my father, "That one's gonna be a priest." I didn't think much of the old man's comment until later in life.

There were family vacations, and then there was life at home in New England, North Dakota. I'll always hold New England close to my heart, especially my parish of St. Mary's. I was brought up a solid Catholic by both of my parents in that parish. Mom would drag all nine of her children off to Mass every day of the week no matter what the weather conditions were. She would make sure that we said a daily rosary, Stations of the Cross, and made a confession at least once a month. Many of our summer First Friday's were spent in front of the Blessed Sacrament instead of swimming like the other kids in town. Other than these monumental tasks, Mother really didn't care much about our faith life.

Dad, on the other hand, would always support Mom by occasionally coming to weekday Mass when he could, and by always praying the rosary with us. He didn't have much to do since he ONLY had to provide for the eleven of us. He worked hard on the farm day after day and hardly got paid for it. He was the city judge on the side. But Dad always had faith and never gave up. His greatest rules were never lie, and to always think what needed to be done for the future. The greatest lessons we learned came from Dad. Since Mom always made the entire family eat supper together, Dad was provided a perfect time to talk about philosophy, play a game he made, or tell Irish jokes to all of us.

Dad was the family stronghold and Mom filled it with love. The other residents:, Bill, Dave, Mary, Beth, Leo, Jimmy, Robert and even Paul, my siblings, proved to be a great help when I needed something. I learned how to work with people and how to have a really good time at the same time. It was not uncommon to hear a friend say, "I sure wish I had some brothers and sisters like yours." I'm not trying to portray my family as one of the top ten families ever (although I bet we would have a running chance at being one); rather I'm saying that people enjoyed our family because we knew how to work with one another and have fun at the same time.

My family played a very important role in my choice to enter the seminary, although I never realized their effect on my life until I went away to college. I had no real focus when leaving home, and no idea where I was headed. I hadn't done any serious planning for college until several days before classes began, and only then did I decide to attend North Dakota State University.

I arrived on campus two days before classes began and started to sign up for courses while most other freshmen were enjoying life on their own. Many of the classes I tried to take were unavailable. It made no difference that the classes were filled because I had no idea

206

what classes I wanted to take anyway. I continued to try to find classes that would fill my time at NDSU, and in desperation I opened a university book of scheduled classes and dug for possibilities. I finally found one that was of interest to me, Latin 110. I decided to take the class on condition that if I couldn't do it I would drop it immediately.

I believe that this Latin class was a sign to help me discern my vocation. How? As I walked into the classroom the first day, about ten guys came dressed a cut above the rest with holy water, crucifixes, and a spirit of happiness. This was to be my first encounter with a group of seminarians. As that first class began, I felt a seed growing in my heart, a desire to be as close to God as they were.

And so my journey to the seminary began. At first God's call was a simple, quiet kind of call. I began to pray a daily rosary, asking Our Blessed Lady what God had in store for my life. Then, I began to attend daily Mass on campus and said prayers constantly during the day as my parents had taught me to do. I realized that I was submitting my way to God's way. As my life grew more intense with God I knew that I had to talk to someone who would understand what I should do with it. There were many nights when I would go to the church on campus and cry, pleading with God: "It would be much easier for the two of us if you just came out of that tabernacle and told me what to do with the rest of my life."

Finally, I asked my oldest brother, Bill, what I should do about it. We had a long talk about it and finally he said, "Look, Jack, I'm not going to tell you what to do with your life. You wouldn't want me to! But you should always be open to what God wants you to do." After the talk with Bill, I felt more confused than ever. However, after I thought about it, it made a lot of sense.

To complicate matters more, I had a girlfriend at the time that I loved very much. Not only did I love her but I was also a very good friend of her family (or at least they lead me to believe that I was). By the time Thanksgiving came around that year, I still had not told her that I was considering entering the seminary. As a matter of fact, I hadn't told anyone except Bill. Somehow, someway, during that Thanksgiving holiday I received my call from God: RRRRRIIIIINNNNNGGGG!!!!!!! "Will someone please get the phone? Hey, Jack, it's for you!"

I suspected the caller to be my girlfriend and said, "Annie?" The unsuspecting caller replied, "No!"

To tell the truth, it didn't even sound like Annie because it wasn't. It was the vocation director of the Bismarck Diocese, the good Monsignor Walsh!!

The good Monsignor had received my name from a program set up to find possible seminarians. He decided to do some "vocationing" while I was "vacationing."

He asked me several questions about school, which I knew had nothing to do with what he was calling about. Finally, he came to the point and asked me if I had ever thought of being a priest. My heart stopped beating for a half hour to an hour. Finally, when I regained consciousness (the good Monsignor had the patience to stay on the line), I explained to him that I really hadn't thought of anything else besides the priesthood since I entered college, and had always wanted to be a priest ever since I could remember.

And so this phone call put a start to my calling in life. My dreams of being a priest had started to take form. Oh, how I had dreamed of being able to offer the Most Holy Sacrifice of the Mass. How I wanted to be close to Jesus like I was when I visited him in the Blessed Sacrament. I embraced the thought of being a priest for God; a life that I knew I could never be worthy of but one that I knew God wanted me to live.

But before this was going to happen, I had to give back to God one of the most wonderful gifts of my life, Annie. After agreeing to become a seminarian over the phone, I immediately began to procrastinate and decided not to tell Annie until I was absolutely sure that this was what I was going to do in my life. Procrastination got the best of me until Christmas. Finally, I came to my senses and drove to Annie's house to tell her. We drove about a mile outside of town onto a hill where we could view the starry night. Needless to say, Annie was very sad and cried for a long time at the news of my choice. However, by the end of the night she told me that she was glad that I was doing what God wanted to do, although she told me she wanted it different in her heart.

My family, on the other hand, had a completely different outlook on my decision. When I told Mom, she gave me a big hug. When I told Dad, he said, "Well it's about time." The rest of the family seemed to follow Dad's comment, acting as if it were nothing out of the ordinary. So I had the support from my entire family as well as my home parish.

St. Mary's is a parish of about 300 people and has been no stranger to vocations to the priesthood and the religious life. Over 50 vocations have come out of the parish since it began in the early 1900s. The parish gave me great support with prayers and money.

Upon entering the seminary, I began to receive letters of encouragement from people everywhere telling me how happy they were that I was answering God's call. The support was overwhelming as I started my new life with God. I was so happy to be doing what God wanted me to do and have so much wonderful support at the same time.

When people ask what made me give up everything I had going for me in life in exchange for God's call, I tell them that it was because the seminary had really good food or because God wanted me to have one of the happiest lives ever.

So how does it all begin? Always remember to pray. It was in falling away from prayer that I lost happiness in my life. It was in my return to prayer that I found it again. A good priest names Father John Corrapi once said that it wasn't until he moved out of the driver's seat of his life and let God take over that he began to find real happiness.

If a person wishes to know the vocation God has planned for them, they need to hand God the keys to their life and completely trust that God will bring them the greatest happiness in life. It is called "doing his will." There is no other way. Why don't you "Come and See?"

EPILOGUE

When all is said and done, in our own hearts, all of us who have been called and chosen continue to ponder the great mystery of our vocations to ordained ministry. In our most serious moments we stand before our God alone and empty, knowing that it is ultimately his love and grace which have made such an incredible difference in our lives.

The reflective words of St. Paul in his First Letter to the Corinthians, Chapter 1, verses 26 to 31, beautifully sum up the sentiments of our honest admissions when he says, *"Brothers, you are among those called. Consider you own situation. Not many of you are wise, as men account wisdom; not many are influential; and surely not many are well-born. God chose those whom the world considers absurd to shame the wise; he singled out the weak of this world to shame the strong. He chose the world's lowborn and despised, those who count for nothing, to reduce to nothing those who were something; so that mankind can do no boasting before God. God it is who has given you life in Christ Jesus. He has made him our wisdom and also our justice, our sanctification, and our redemption. This is just as you find it written, 'Let him who would boast, boast in the Lord.'"*

And as I said in the beginning, "Funes caeciderunt mihi in amoena, et heretitatis mea perplacet mihi." (Psalm 15:6).